Introduction

Reading comprehension can be practiced and improved in the context of informational reading, as well as in the reading students do every day in the course of their daily lives. This book presents environmental print in the context of scenes and other print media, along with short stories of explanation. The topics chosen include familiar settings and experiences, while at the same time introducing new vocabulary and ideas to children.

A page of questions follows each story. These questions will provide a child familiarity with different types of test questions. In addition, the practice they provide will help a child develop good testing skills. Questions are written so that they lead a child to focus on what was read. They provide practice for finding the main idea, as well as specific details. They provide practice in deciphering new and unknown vocabulary words. In addition, the questions encourage a child to think beyond the facts. For example, every question set has an analogy question where students are expected to think about the relationship between two things and find a pair of words with the same type of relationship. Other questions provide an opportunity for the child to infer and consider possible consequences relevant to the information provided in the story.

The book is designed so that writing can be incorporated into every lesson. The level of writing will depend on what the teacher desires, as well as the needs of the child.

Lessons in *Nonfiction Reading Comprehension: Informational Reading* meet and are correlated to the Mid-continent Research for Education and Learning (McREL) standards. They are listed on page 8.

A place for *Nonfiction Reading Comprehension: Informational Reading* can be found in every classroom or home. It can be a part of daily instruction in time designated for reading or other academic areas as specific topics of study relate to the stories presented. It can be used for both group and individual instruction. Stories can be read with someone or on one's own. *Nonfiction Reading Comprehension: Informational Reading* can help children improve in multiple areas, including reading, critical thinking, writing, and test-taking.

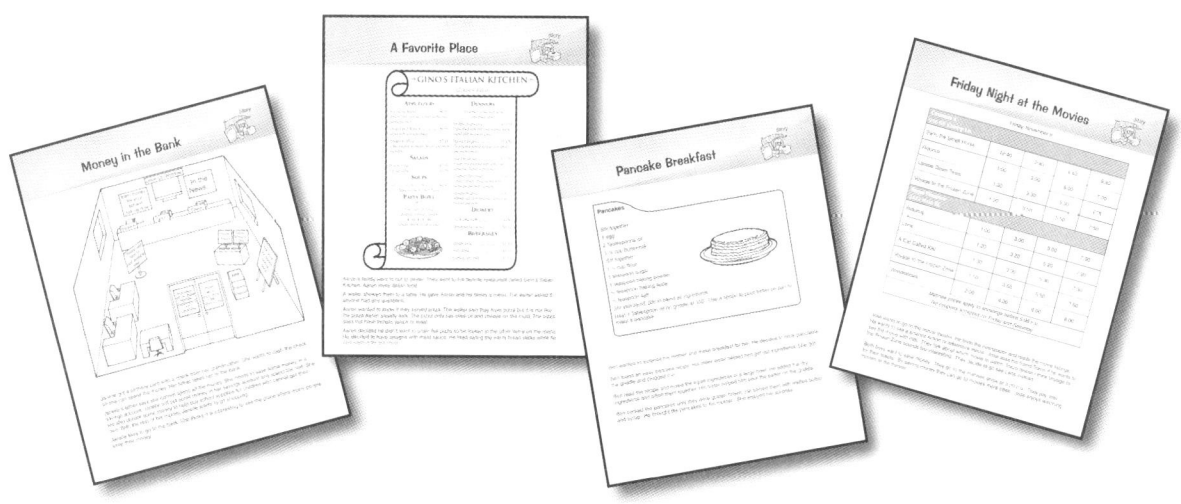

Using this Book

The Stories

Each story in *Nonfiction Reading Comprehension: Informational Reading* is a separate unit. For this reason, the stories can but do not have to be read in order. A teacher can choose any story that matches classroom activity.

Stories can be assigned to be read during reading or other related academic periods. They can be used as classroom work or supplemental material.

Each story contains a scene or sample of environmental print as well as a short story of explanation. They range from 50 to 200 words in length. They are written at grade level with elementary sentence structure.

New Words

Each story is provided with a list of eight vocabulary words. These words may be used in the short story or the environmental scene. New words may sometimes have an addition of a simple word ending such as "s," "ed," or "ing." Many of the new words are found in more than one story. Mastery of the new words may not come immediately, but practice articulating, seeing, and writing the words will build a foundation for future learning.

* A teacher may choose to have the children read and repeat the words together as a class.

* While it is true that the majority of the words are defined explicitly or in context of the stories, a teacher may choose to discuss and define the new words before the children start reading. This will only reinforce word identification and reading vocabulary.

* A teacher may engage the class in an activity where children use the new word in a sentence. Or, the teacher may use the word in two sentences. Only one sentence will use the word correctly. Children will be asked to identify which sentence is correct. For example, one new word is "focus". The teacher might say,

    "The focus of the project is teamwork."

    "They used a focus to find their way."

* A teacher may also allow children to choose one new word to add to their weekly spelling list. This provides children with an opportunity to feel part of a decision-making process, as well as to gain "ownership" over new words.

In addition, practice spelling new words reinforces the idea that we can learn to recognize new words across stories because there is consistency in spelling.

* A teacher may choose to have children go through the story after it is read and circle each new word.

Editor
Andrea Tropeano, M.A.

Managing Editor
Ina Massler Levin, M.A.

Illustrator
Howard Cheney

Cover Artist
Courtney Barnes

Art Coordinator
Renée Christine Yates

Art Production Manager
Kevin Barnes

Imaging
Nathan P. Rivera

Publisher
Mary D. Smith, M.S. Ed.

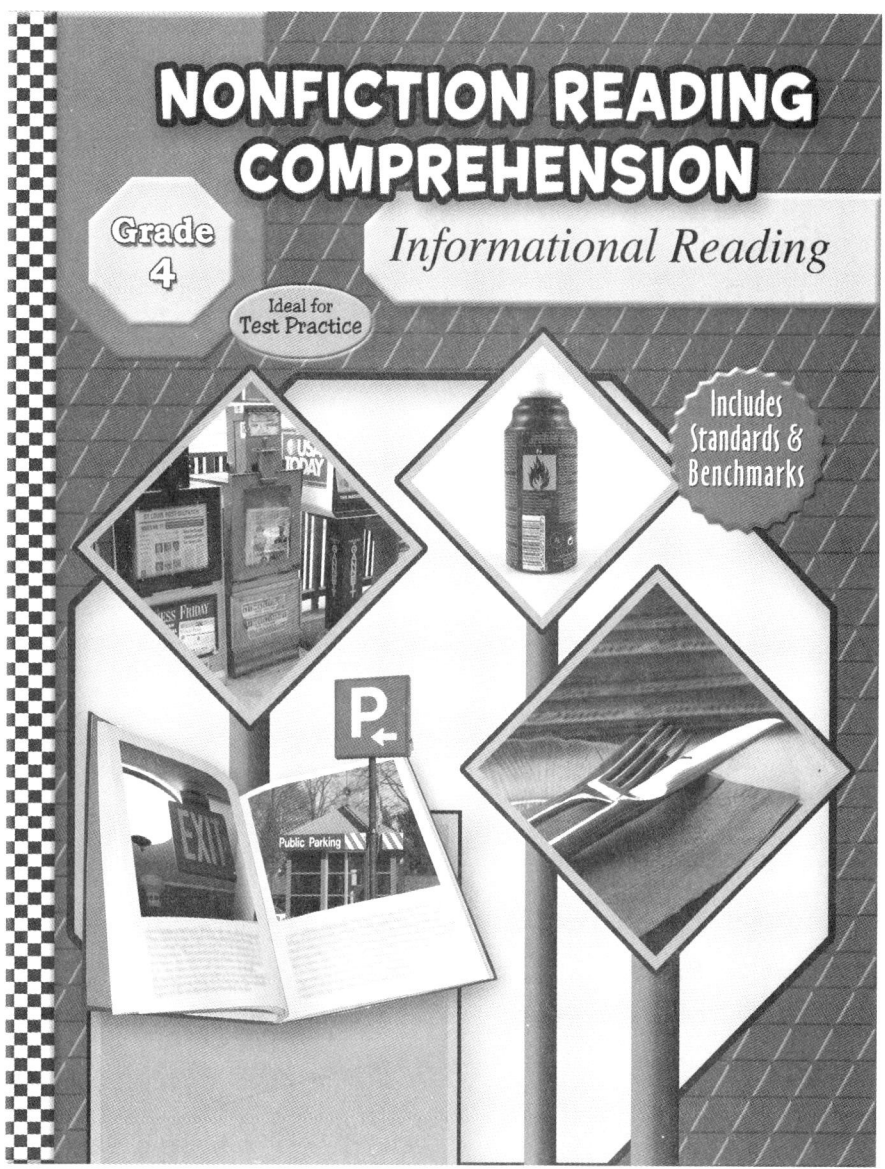

Author
Tracie Heskett, M.Ed.

The classroom teacher may reproduce copies of materials in this book for classroom use only. Reproduction of any part for an entire school or school system is strictly prohibited. No part of this publication may be transmitted, stored, or recorded in any form without written permission from the publisher.

Teacher Created Resources, Inc.
6421 Industry Way
Westminster, CA 92683
www.teachercreated.com
ISBN: 978-1-4206-8864-1:
© 2007 Teacher Created Resources, Inc.
Made in U.S.A.

Table of Contents

Introduction 3
Using This Book 4
  The Stories
  New Words
  The Writing Link
  The Questions
  The Test Link
  Environmental Print
Meeting Standards 8
Reading Stories
  Rafael Needs Shoes 9
  Money in the Bank....................................12
  Grocery Shopping 15
  Going to the Airport...................................18
  A New Skateboard 21
  A Night at the Theater 24
  A Favorite Place 27
  Teamwork 30
  Reminder from Mom..................................33
  Scout Camp..36
  Party Time 39
  State Report 42
  First Day 45
  Build a Kite 48
  Pancake Breakfast.....................................51
  Crazy Hair 54
  Adopt a Pet 57
  Stay Healthy 60
  Getting Ready for Fall................................63
  Movie Time 66
  Summer Plans 69
  Winter Holiday Concert 72
  Gymnastics Class......................................75
  Visit a Volcano 78
  Fair Days 81
  Friday Night at the Movies........................84
  Computer Fun 87
  Four Wheeling 90
  A Modern Artist 93
  Technology in the News 96
  Anthology of Folk Tales 99
  Learning New Science Words 102
  At the Lake 105
  Exploring the Library 108
  Shopping Day 111
  The World Around Us................................114
  Steven's New School 117
  Sunday Bike Ride 120
  Camp Woodleaf 123
  Make a Hamburger....................................126
  Guess My Word 129
  Challenge 132
  Settling the West 135
  Young Rabbit's Journey.............................138
Answer Sheets...141
Answer Key 142

Using this Book *(cont.)*

The Writing Link

* A teacher may choose to link writing exercises to the stories presented in the book. All writing links reinforce handwriting and spelling skills. Writing links with optional sentence tasks reinforce sentence construction and punctuation.

* A teacher may choose to have a child pick one new word from the list of new words and write it out. Space for the word write-out is provided in this book. This option may seem simple, but it provides a child with an opportunity to take control. The child is not overwhelmed by the task of the word write-out because the child is choosing the word. It also reinforces sight-word identification. If a teacher has begun to instruct children in cursive writing, the teacher can ask the child to write out the word twice, once in print, and once in cursive.

* A teacher may choose to have a child write out a complete sentence using one of the new words. The sentences can be formulated together as a class, or as individual work. Depending on other classroom work, the teacher may want to remind children about capital letters and ending punctuation.

* A teacher may require a child to write out a sentence after the story questions have been answered. The sentence may or may not contain a new word. The sentence may have one of the following starts:

  - I learned…
  - I thought…
  - Did you know…
  - An interesting thing about…

If a teacher decides on this type of sentence formation, the teacher may want to show children how they can use words directly from the story to help form their sentences, as well as make sure that words in their sentences are not misspelled. For example, this is the first paragraph in the selection titled "Build a Kite."

Nathan's dad collects different kinds of kites. He taught Nathan how to build a kite called a sled. It is made from a large black plastic trash bag.

Possible sample sentence write-outs may be

"I learned that some people collect kites."
"I thought that you could only make a kite out of paper."
"Did you know one kind of kite is called a sled?"
"An interesting thing about kites is that you can build your own."

This type of exercise reinforces spelling and sentence structure. It also teaches a child responsibility—a child learns to go back to the story to check word spelling. It also provides elementary report writing skills. Students are taking information from a story source and reporting it in their own sentence construction.

Using this Book (cont.)

The Questions

Five questions follow every story. Questions always contain one main idea, specific detail, and analogy question.

* The main idea question pushes a child to focus on the topic of what was read. It allows practice in discerning between answers that are too broad or narrow.

* The specific detail question requires a child to retrieve or recall a particular fact mentioned in the story. Children gain practice referring back to a source. They also are pushed to think about the structure of the story. Where would this fact most likely be mentioned in the story? What paragraph or part of the scene would most likely contain the fact they are retrieving?

* The analogy question pushes a child to develop reasoning skills. It pairs two words mentioned in the story or scene and asks the child to think about how the words relate to each other. A child is then asked to find an analogous pair. Children are expected to recognize and use analogies in all course readings, written work, and listening. This particular type of question is found on many cognitive-functioning tests.

* The remaining two questions are a mixture of vocabulary, inference, or sequencing questions. Going back and reading the word in context can help answer vocabulary questions. The inference and sequencing questions provide practice for what students will find on standardized tests. They also encourage a child to think beyond the story. They push a child to think critically about how facts can be interpreted.

The Test Link

Standardized tests have become obligatory in schools throughout our nation and the world. There are certain test-taking skills and strategies that can be developed by using *Nonfiction Reading Comprehension: Informational Reading*.

* Questions can be answered on the page by filling in the bubble. You may also choose to have students fill in bubbles on a teacher created answer sheet. Filling in the bubble pages provides practice responding in a standardized-test format.

* Questions are presented in a mixed up order, though the main-idea question is always among the first three. The analogy question is always one of the last three. This mixed up order provides practice with standardized test formats, where though reading comprehension passages often have main-idea questions, the main-idea question is not necessarily placed first.

Using this Book (cont.)

The Test Link (cont.)

* A teacher may want to point out to students that often a main idea question can be used to help a child focus on what the story is about. A teacher may also want to point out that an analogy question can be done any time, as it is not crucial to the main focus of the story.

* A teacher may want to reinforce that a child should read every answer choice. Many children are afraid of not remembering information. Reinforcing this tip helps a child to remember that on multiple-choice tests, one is *identifying* the best answer, not making an answer up.

* A teacher may choose to discuss the strategy of eliminating wrong answer choices to find the correct one. Teachers should instruct children that even if they can only eliminate one answer choice, their guess will have a better chance of being right. A teacher may want to go through several questions to demonstrate this strategy. For example, in the story scene "Make a Hamburger," there is the question:

> 2. This story is mainly about
>
> Ⓐ a barbecue   Ⓒ a list of food items
>
> Ⓑ a hamburger card game   Ⓓ a group of boys

Although a hamburger, food items, and the group of boys are mentioned in the story, there is no mention of a barbecue. A child may be able to eliminate that answer choice immediately. A guess at this point has a better chance of being correct than when there were four choices to choose from. A teacher can remind children, too, that there is the option of going back and finding the parts of the story with the words *hamburger, item,* and *boys* in them. The story refers to items and the boys. In fact, they appear to have equal weight. As one cannot be a better choice than the other, neither one of them can be correct.

Environmental Print

The term "environmental print" refers to the printed words children see every day in the world around them. These words may be on signs, posters, containers, or buildings. Children read environmental print at home, in the classroom, stores, other places in the community, and outdoors. They also encounter print on a regular basis on directions, maps, and various types of schedules. Children become very familiar with the words they see every day and can often read much more than others realize. Practice reading for information in non-manuscript format allows children to gain confidence in their reading comprehension and test-taking abilities as they encounter print with which they are already familiar.

Meeting Standards

Listed below are the McREL standards for language arts Level 2 (grades 3–5). All standards and benchmarks are used with permission from McREL.

> Copyright 2004 McREL
> Mid-continent Research for Education and Learning
> 2550 S. Parker Road, Suite 500
> Aurora, CO 80014
> Telephone: (303) 337-0990
> Website: *www.mcrel.org/standards-benchmarks*

McREL Standards are in **bold**. Benchmarks are in regular print. All lessons meet the following standards and benchmarks unless noted.

Uses stylistic and rhetorical aspects of writing

- Uses a variety of sentence structures in writing (*All lessons where writing a complete sentence option is followed*)
- Uses grammatical and mechanical conventions in written compositions
- Writes in cursive (*All lessons where teacher follows the option of writing a sentence using a new word or completion of beginning sentence options in cursive*)
- Uses conventions of spelling, capitalization, and punctuation in writing compositions (*All lessons where teacher follows option of writing a sentence using a new word or completion of beginning sentence options*)

Uses the general skills and strategies of the reading process

- Previews text
- Establishes a purpose for reading
- Represents concrete information as explicit mental pictures
- Uses phonetic and structural analysis techniques, syntactic structure, and semantic context to decode unknown words
- Uses a variety of context clues to decode unknown words
- Understands level-appropriate reading vocabulary
- Monitors own reading strategies and makes modifications as needed
- Adjust speed of reading to suit purpose and difficulty of material
- Understands the author's purpose

Uses reading skills and strategies to understand a variety of informational texts

- Summarizes and paraphrases information in texts
- Uses prior knowledge and experience to understand and respond to new information

Rafael Needs Shoes

New Words

These are new words to practice.
Say each word 10 times.

* formal
* casual
* court
* size

* sale
* pair
* fit
* lace

Choose one new word to write.

_____

- -

_____

Rafael Needs Shoes

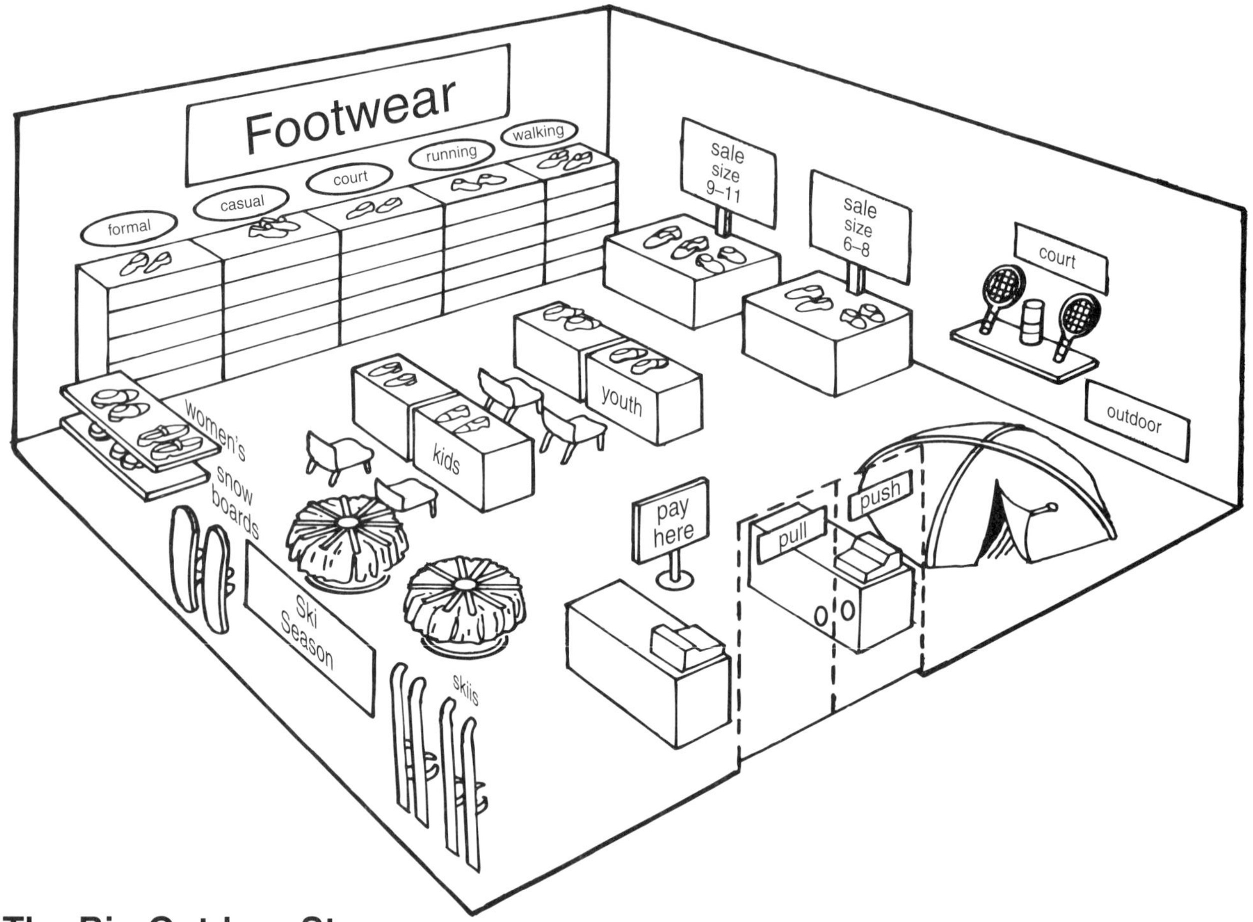

The Big Outdoor Store

Rafael needed a new pair of shoes. He wanted some shoes he could wear to play basketball. Rafael and his mom went to the sporting goods store that sells shoes and sports equipment.

Rafael found the footwear department. He looked at the shoe display. Youth shoes were in the center aisle but he needed a larger size. Rafael looked at all the different types of shoes. The casual tennis shoes didn't look sturdy enough to use for running and jumping. He knew he didn't need formal footwear for basketball. He looked at shoes for running and for walking. His mother said he should look at the court shoes. Rafael found a pair of court shoes that he liked. His mother helped him measure his feet on a measuring device in the store. A salesman got his size from the back storage room and Rafael tried them on. He walked around the store to see if the shoes felt comfortable.

His mother asked him to look at the sale tables to see if any basketball shoes were on sale. Rafael found a nice pair of black and red high tops with rubber soles but they weren't basketball shoes.

Rafael still had the box of shoes that he tried on. He checked that the new pair of shoes had a left shoe and a right shoe. He laced up the shoes so he could wear them home. His mother walked to the front counter and paid for the shoes.

Rafael Needs Shoes

Quiz

Look at the picture. Read the story.
Use the picture and the story to answer the questions.

1. Rafael needed to know what size shoes to buy. He needed to know
   - ⓐ what color socks to wear
   - ⓑ the measurement of his foot
   - ⓒ what kind of shoes to buy
   - ⓓ the length of the shoelaces

2. This story is mainly about
   - ⓐ walking around a store
   - ⓑ going skiing
   - ⓒ running a race
   - ⓓ buying shoes

3. Think about how the word *left* relates to the word *right*. Which words relate in the same way?

   left : right

   - ⓐ pair : shoes
   - ⓑ above : top
   - ⓒ formal : casual
   - ⓓ youth : kids

4. Where will Rafael find the running shoes?
   - ⓐ next to walking shoes
   - ⓑ next to casual shoes
   - ⓒ next to formal shoes
   - ⓓ next to women's shoes

5. When might Rafael need formal shoes?
   - ⓐ to go to school
   - ⓑ to go to a wedding
   - ⓒ to play outside
   - ⓓ to go to the library

Money in the Bank

New Words

These are new words to practice.
Say each word 10 times.

- earn
- teller
- express
- deposit
- withdrawal
- save
- cash
- account

Choose one new word to write.

Money in the Bank

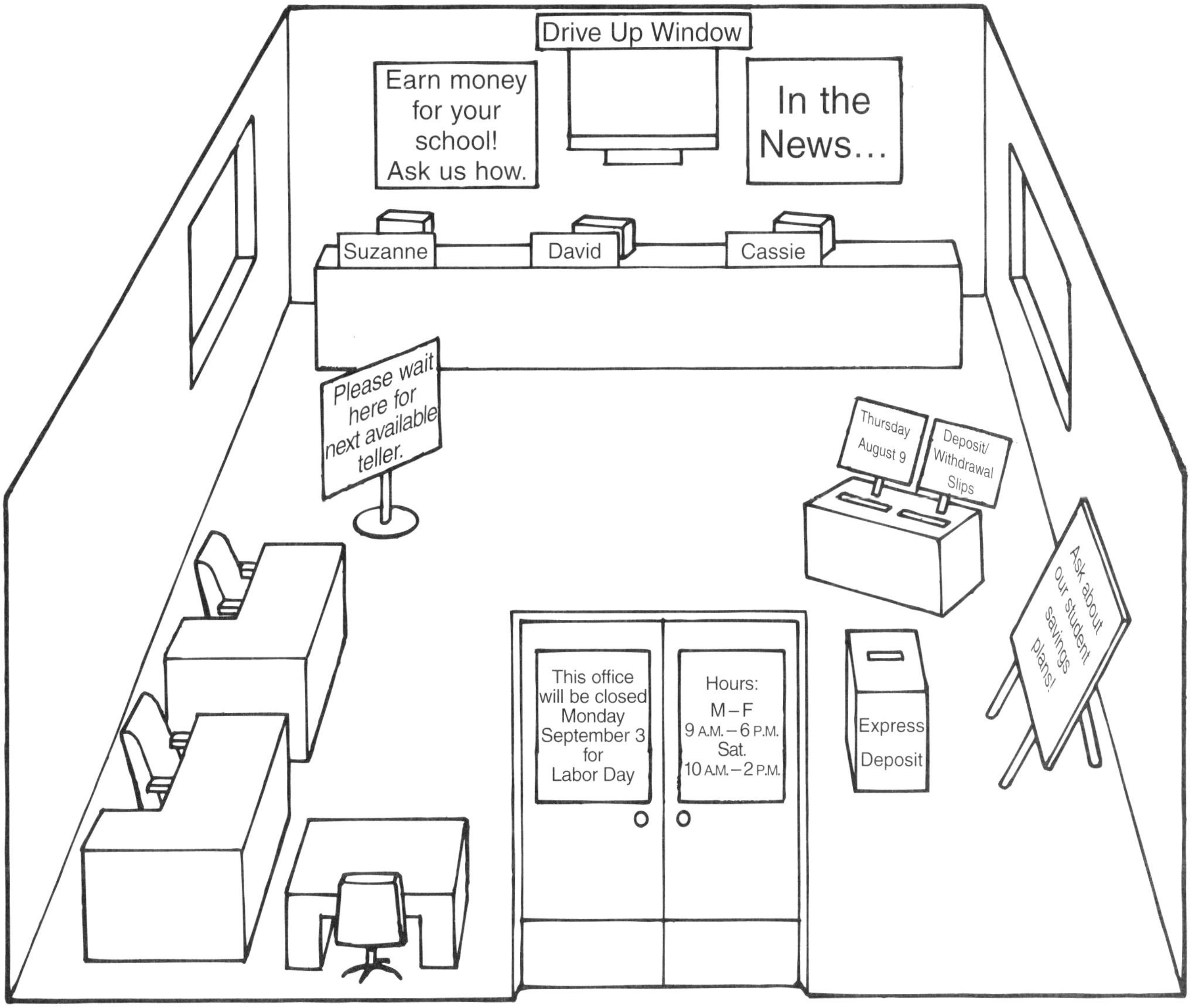

Story

Janelle got a birthday card with a check from her grandmother. She wants to cash the check so she can spend the money. Her father takes her to the bank.

Janelle's father says she cannot spend all the money. She needs to save some money in a savings account. Janelle will put some money in her savings account and spend the rest. She will also donate some money to help buy school supplies for children who cannot get their own. With the rest of her money, Janelle wants to go shopping.

Janelle likes to go to the bank. She thinks it is interesting to see the place where many people keep their money.

Money in the Bank

Quiz

Look at the picture. Read the story.

Use the picture and the story to answer the questions.

1. What kind of person will help Janelle?

   Ⓐ a manager
   Ⓑ a parent
   Ⓒ a teller
   Ⓓ a teacher

2. Which paper will Janelle need to write on to put money in the bank?

   Ⓐ a deposit slip
   Ⓑ a withdrawal slip
   Ⓒ the newspaper
   Ⓓ a student savings plan

3. This story is mainly about

   Ⓐ Janelle's birthday party
   Ⓑ going to the bank
   Ⓒ Janelle's grandmother
   Ⓓ spending money

4. How could Janelle put money in the bank without standing in line?

   Ⓐ give it to her father
   Ⓑ put it into a piggy bank
   Ⓒ use the express deposit
   Ⓓ leave it under the door

5. Think about how the word *withdrawal* relates to the word *deposit*. Which words relate in the same way?

   withdrawal : deposit

   Ⓐ fast : express
   Ⓑ student : school
   Ⓒ teller : bank
   Ⓓ save : spend

Grocery Shopping

New Words

**These are new words to practice.
Say each word 10 times.**

- service
- allow
- pasta
- bulk
- poultry
- supplies
- beverage
- grocery

Choose one new word to write.

_____

- -

_____

Grocery Shopping

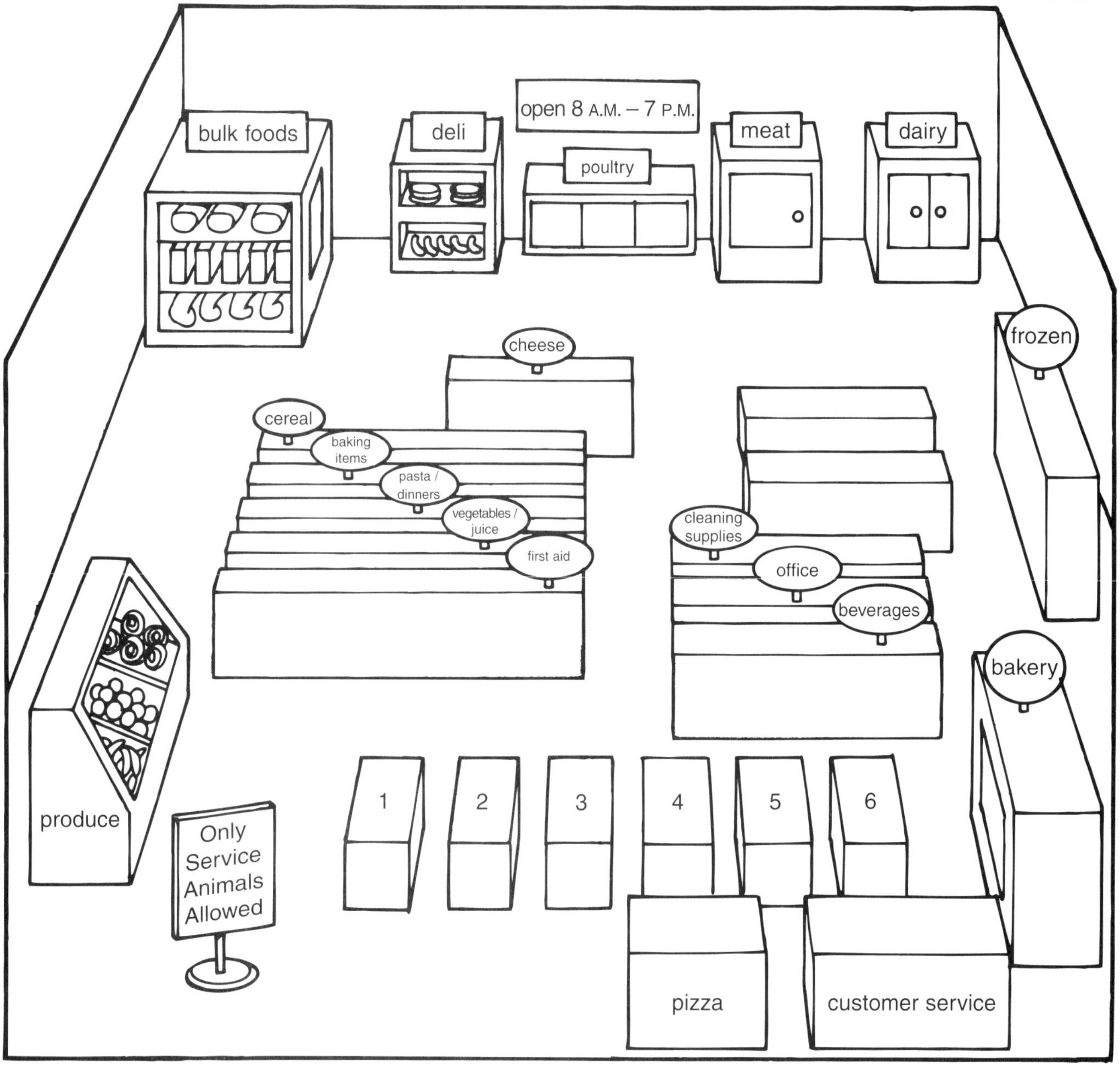

Story

Anna went to the store with her mother to get food for breakfast and lunch. Anna will help her mother bake bread when they get home.

To make bread they needed to get a lot of flour. This store has a bulk foods department. Anna's mother could get as much flour as she needed in this department.

For breakfast they got some cereal. They got fruit and yogurt for lunch. Anna's mother said they needed water so they went to the beverage aisle. They got everything they needed on their list. They went to the checkout counter and Anna's mother paid for their groceries.

#8864 Informational Reading ©Teacher Created Resources, Inc.

Grocery Shopping

Quiz

Look at the picture. Read the story.

Use the picture and the story to answer the questions.

1. This story is mainly about

    Ⓐ eating lunch

    Ⓑ getting yogurt

    Ⓒ making bread

    Ⓓ buying groceries

2. Anna's mother wants lunch meat from the deli. When can she go to the store?

    Ⓐ 7:00 A.M.

    Ⓑ 9:30 A.M.

    Ⓒ 7:30 P.M.

    Ⓓ 8:00 P.M.

3. Anna helped her mother make bread. Where did they get the flour?

    Ⓐ in the bulk foods section

    Ⓑ at the bakery

    Ⓒ on the pasta aisle

    Ⓓ in the cereal aisle

4. Think about how the word *poultry* relates to the word *meat*. Which words relate in the same way?

    poultry : meat

    Ⓐ fruit : vegetable

    Ⓑ yogurt : dairy

    Ⓒ bulk : bakery

    Ⓓ service : animal

5. Anna got a *beverage*. She got

    Ⓐ something frozen

    Ⓑ something to drink

    Ⓒ a snack

    Ⓓ something for cleaning

©Teacher Created Resources, Inc.   #8864 Informational Reading

Going to the Airport

New Words

**These are new words to practice.
Say each word 10 times.**

- security
- maintain
- control
- luggage

- airline
- baggage
- claim
- terminal

Choose one new word to write.

_____

- -

_____

Going to the Airport

Story

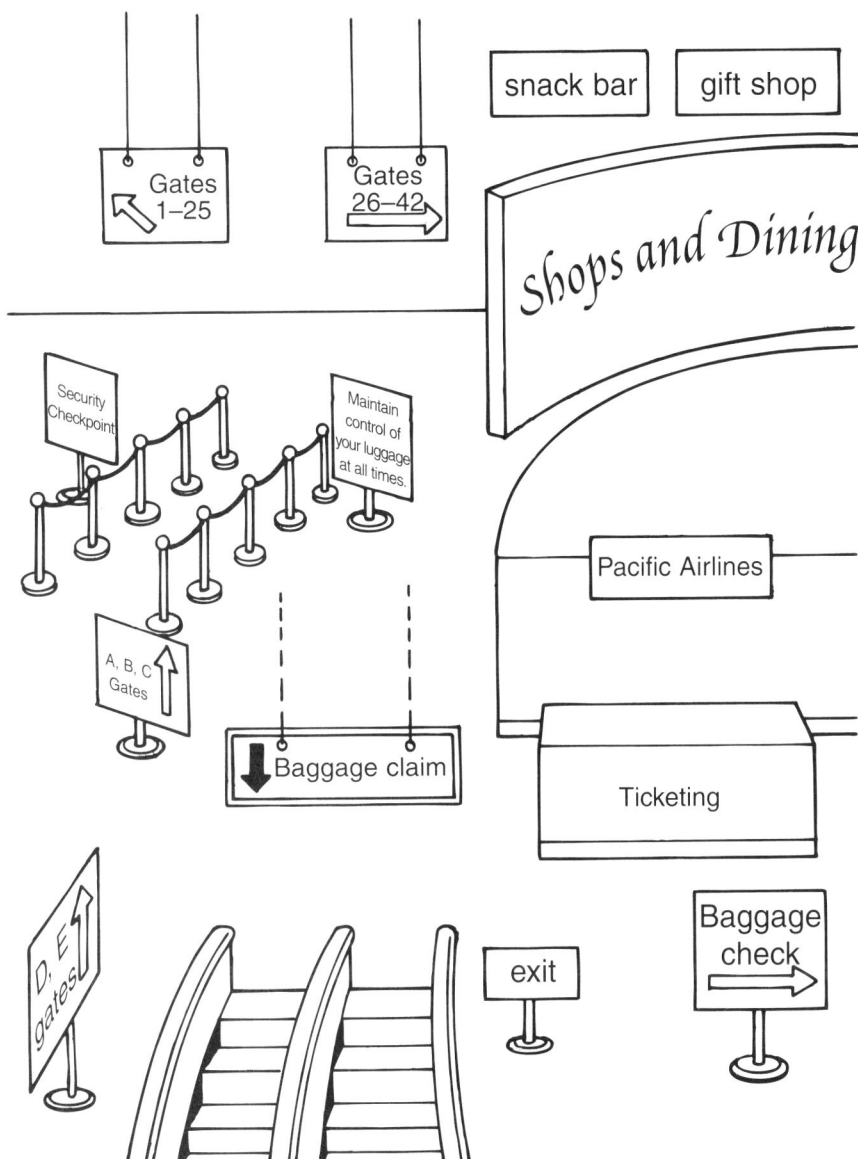

Ken's family is going on vacation. They will travel on an airplane. On the day of their trip, they wake up early and arrive at the airport terminal to check in.

Ken stands in line at the ticketing counter. He will check in his suitcase. He gives it to an airline attendant. He keeps his backpack to take with him on the plane.

Ken's family got their tickets and now they must go through security. They stand in line again. Ken takes off his shoes and puts them in a plastic bin on the moving belt. He also puts his backpack on the belt. His things go through an x-ray machine. Ken's family clears security and heads towards the gates.

The tickets say their aircraft will depart from gate 28. Ken walks through the airport and looks around. He likes to watch the airplanes as he looks out the big glass windows.

Going to the Airport

Quiz

Look at the picture. Read the story.

Use the picture and the story to answer the questions.

1. What will Ken do before he goes to the gate?
    - Ⓐ claim his suitcase
    - Ⓑ get on the airplane
    - Ⓒ go through the security checkpoint
    - Ⓓ go shopping

2. Ken checks his *baggage*. He checks his
    - Ⓐ suitcase
    - Ⓑ shopping bags
    - Ⓒ coat
    - Ⓓ computer

3. This story is mainly about
    - Ⓐ an airplane
    - Ⓑ an airport
    - Ⓒ a vacation
    - Ⓓ a backpack

4. What should Ken not do?
    - Ⓐ go through security
    - Ⓑ take off his shoes
    - Ⓒ open his backpack
    - Ⓓ give his backpack to someone else

5. Think about how the word *baggage* relates to the word *luggage*. Which words relate in the same way?

    baggage : luggage

    - Ⓐ airport : terminal
    - Ⓑ claim : check
    - Ⓒ airplane : aircraft
    - Ⓓ arrive : depart

#8864 Informational Reading

A New Skateboard

New Words

These are new words to practice.
Say each word 10 times.

* experience
* thrill
* adventure
* aerial

* detach
* convert
* advertisement
* helmet

Choose one new word to write.

_____

- -

_____

Story

A New Skateboard

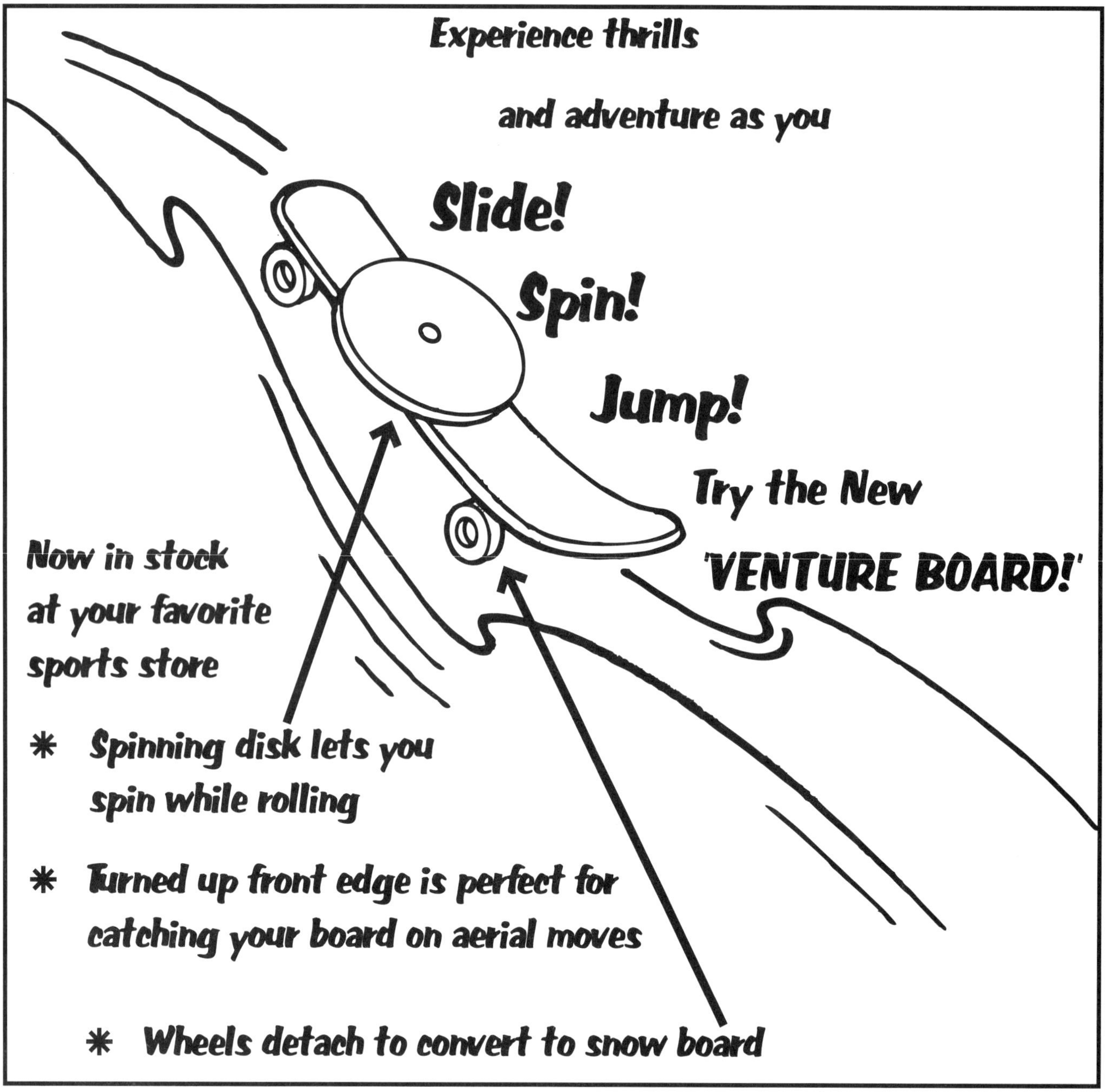

Experience thrills and adventure as you

Slide!

Spin!

Jump!

Try the New 'VENTURE BOARD!'

Now in stock at your favorite sports store

* **Spinning disk lets you spin while rolling**
* **Turned up front edge is perfect for catching your board on aerial moves**
* **Wheels detach to convert to snow board**

Jordan saw this skateboard advertisement in a magazine. His friend has a skateboard that Jordan sometimes borrows to ride. His friend's skateboard is not like the one in the advertisement.

Jordan reads the ad and thinks it would be fun to spin and go downhill at the same time. He wants to find out how much this skateboard costs so he goes to a sports store.

Jordan talks to a clerk at the store about the skateboard. He finds out the board costs $40. Jordan will have to save some money before he can buy one. He will need to buy a helmet, too. The person at the store says this skateboard is exciting to ride.

A New Skateboard

Quiz

Look at the picture. Read the story.

Use the picture and the story to answer the questions.

1. Jordan can do *aerial* moves. He can ride the skateboard
   - Ⓐ on the ground
   - Ⓑ in the air
   - Ⓒ down a hill
   - Ⓓ on the snow

2. This story is mainly about
   - Ⓐ a snowboard
   - Ⓑ a bicycle
   - Ⓒ a skateboard advertisement
   - Ⓓ a magazine

3. Think about how the word *wheel* relates to the word *skateboard*. Which words relate in the same way?

   | wheel : skateboard |

   - Ⓐ thrill : adventure
   - Ⓑ spin : jump
   - Ⓒ cost : money
   - Ⓓ bindings : snowboard

4. Why does Jordan need to wear a helmet when riding the skateboard?
   - Ⓐ to keep from getting injured
   - Ⓑ to look like a skateboarder
   - Ⓒ to keep his head warm
   - Ⓓ to listen to music

5. How did Jordan find out how much the board costs?
   - Ⓐ he read the magazine
   - Ⓑ he went to the sports store
   - Ⓒ he asked his friend
   - Ⓓ he looked on the Internet

A Night at the Theater

New Words

These are new words to practice.
Say each word 10 times.

- play
- stage
- auditorium
- comedy
- refreshments
- audition
- rehearsal
- drama

Choose one new word to write.

A Night at the Theater

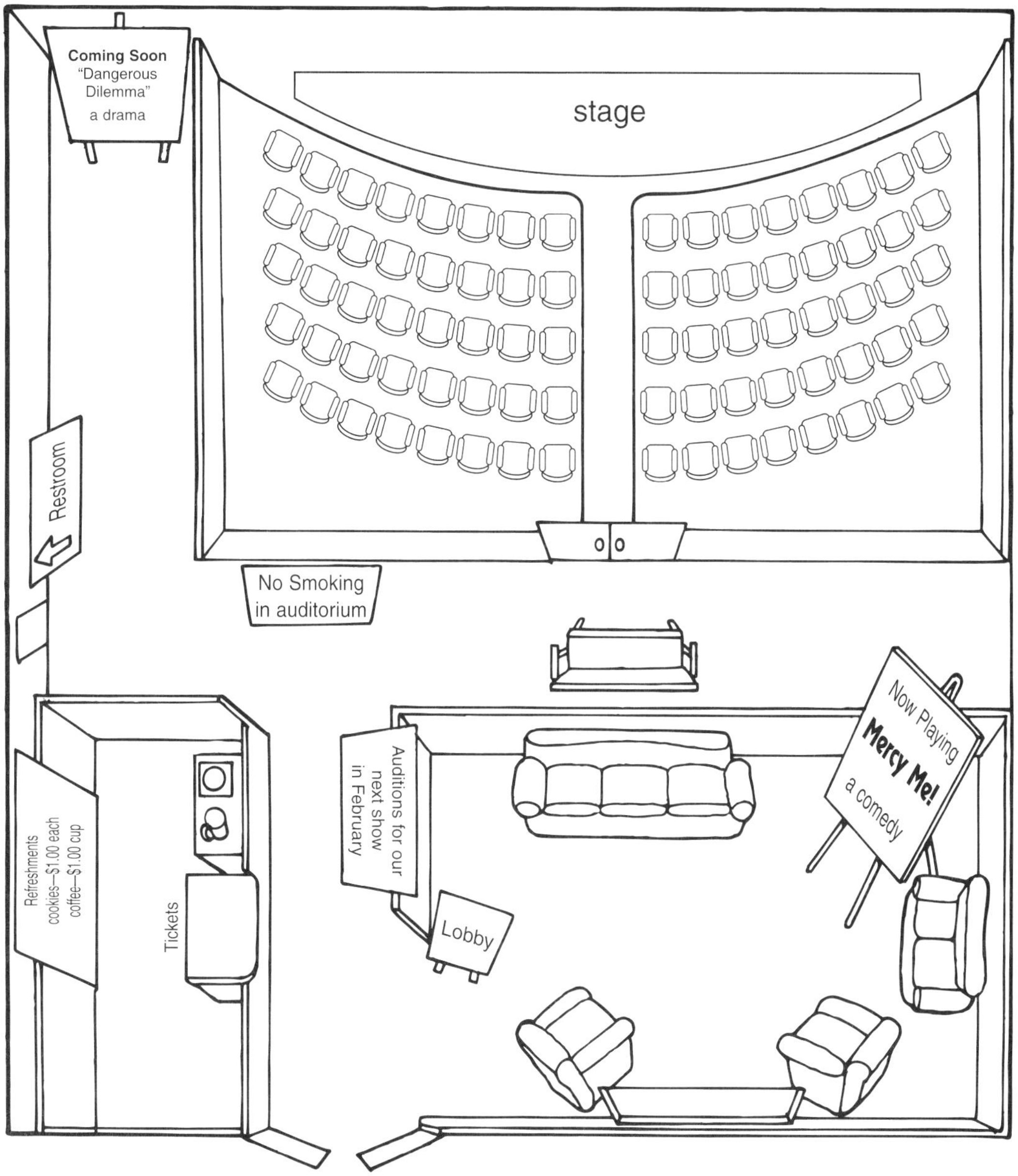

Story

Greta and her parents went to see a play. They went to a small theater. The play they chose to see is a comedy.

Greta's parents paid for the tickets. They bought 3 cookies at the refreshment stand. Greta sat in the lobby and ate her cookie while she waited for the show to begin.

She read the posters on the walls. One poster described the show Greta's family would see. Another poster gave information about auditions for the next show. Greta wondered if children could try out to be in the play.

Greta and her family went into the auditorium and found their seats. They thought the play was funny and entertaining. At the end of the show, they clapped for the actors.

A Night at the Theater

Quiz

Look at the picture. Read the story.

Use the picture and the story to answer the questions.

1. Where will the actors perform?

    A. on the stage
    B. at the ticket counter
    C. in the lobby
    D. at the audition

2. What kind of play did Greta's family see?

    A. a drama
    B. a comedy
    C. a musical
    D. an action adventure

3. This story is mainly about

    A. the theater
    B. the playground
    C. the refreshments
    D. the actors

4. Greta may get some *refreshments*. She may get

    A. some water in the sink
    B. a fan because it is hot
    C. something to eat and drink
    D. a rehearsal

5. Think about how the word *comedy* relates to *funny*. Which words relate in the same way?

    comedy : funny

    A. play : drama
    B. cookies : coffee
    C. drama : serious
    D. audition : rehearsal

Favorite Place

New Words

**These are new words to practice.
Say each word 10 times.**

- appetizer
- pasta
- marinara
- sauce
- soup
- herb
- seasoning
- olive

Choose one new word to write.

_____

- - - - - - - - - - - - - - - - - - -

_____

A Favorite Place

GINO'S ITALIAN KITCHEN
Garden Fresh

Appetizers

Foccaccia Bread.........................$6.95
brushed with olive oil, roasted garlic, and parmesan cheese.

Deep Fried Ravioli....................$6.95
served with marinara sauce.

Antipasto Plate.........................$7.95
a fine selection of meats, cheeses, and fresh vegetables.

Salads

House salad...............................$2.95
Caesar salad..............................$3.95

Soups

cup.........$3.50   bowl.........$4.95
Minestrone • Ziti • Pasta

Pasta Bowl
$8.95

*Your choice of pasta:
spaghetti, fettucini, rigatoni
Your choice of sauce:
alfredo, marinara, meat sauce*

Dinners

All dinners served with salad and bread sticks

Stuffed Manicotti....................$13.95
Pasta filled with beef and romano cheese. served with marinara sauce

Baked Lasagna.........................$12.95
Oven baked layered lasagna with meat and ricotta cheese.

Veal Parmesan.........................$15.95
Tender veal seasoned with herbs and parmesan. Baked to perfection.

Chicken Parmesan...................$14.95
Grilled chicken breast topped with parmesan and herb seasoning.

Shrimp Scampi........................$16.50
Shrimp and fresh vegetables sautéed in olive oil and herbs

Dessert

Chocolate torte..........................$4.50
Spumoni ice cream...................$3.50

Beverages

Italian soda................................$2.50
Soft drinks.................................$1.95
Coffee, tea, milk........................$1.75

Aaron's family went to out to dinner. They went to his favorite restaurant called Gino's Italian Kitchen. Aaron loves Italian food.

A waiter showed them to a table. He gave Aaron and his family a menu. The waiter asked if anyone had any questions.

Aaron wanted to know if they served pizza. The waiter said they have pizza but it is not like the pizza Aaron usually eats. The pizza only has olive oil and cheese on the crust. The pizza does not have tomato sauce or meat.

Aaron decided he didn't want to order the pizza so he looked at the other items on the menu. He decided to have lasagna with meat sauce. He liked eating the warm bread sticks while he was waiting for his meal.

A Favorite Place

Quiz

Read the menu. Read the story.

Use the menu and the story to answer the questions.

1. This story is mainly about

    Ⓐ making soup
    Ⓑ eating pizza
    Ⓒ going to a restaurant
    Ⓓ cooking vegetables

2. If Aaron orders a dinner, what will be served with his meal?

    Ⓐ beverage and dessert
    Ⓑ soup and salad
    Ⓒ salad and bread sticks
    Ⓓ appetizer and bread sticks

3. Think about how the word *spaghetti* relates to the word *pasta*. Which words relate in the same way?

    spaghetti : pasta

    Ⓐ minestrone : soup
    Ⓑ salad : bread
    Ⓒ appetizer : dessert
    Ⓓ menu : restaurant

4. Many dishes have *herb* seasoning. An *herb* is

    Ⓐ a person who wears a hat
    Ⓑ a plant used in cooking
    Ⓒ medicine that does not taste good
    Ⓓ a pan used to cook food

5. What will Aaron do with the menu?

    Ⓐ memorize it
    Ⓑ set it aside
    Ⓒ color it
    Ⓓ read it and choose something to eat

Teamwork

New Words

**These are new words to practice.
Say each word 10 times.**

* model   * role

* benefit   * organize

* focus   * include

* team   * original

Choose one new word to write.

Teamwork

Story

Your group will build a model. Your model may be of a historical place, a place in the community, or technology that benefits people in the community.

The main focus of this project is to work together as a team. Each group must decide what role each person will fill. Each group will also need to decide how to organize your project.

Your project must include:

- a list of the names and roles of each group member
- a list of materials needed
- three note cards that describe:
  a) what the model is
  b) why the model is important
  c) details about the model

You will be given points based on neatness, creativity, and original work.

Craig's class is learning how to work in groups. They have learned about many different communities. Craig's teacher gave the class an assignment for a group project. Craig will work with three other students. They decide that Craig will fill the role of note-taker. He will write down what everyone in the group will do. He will write a list of materials and take notes on the group discussions. He will also write information on the three note cards.

The group decides who will gather the materials. They also choose someone to do the artwork. Each group is responsible for presenting their project to the class. They choose someone to speak in front of the class. The members of Craig's group will build the model together.

Teamwork

Quiz

Read the directions. Read the story.

Use the directions and the story to answer the questions.

1. This story is mainly about

    A) making a project at home
    B) how to build a model
    C) working as a team
    D) building a house

2. What is one thing Craig's group will need to do?

    A) paint their model
    B) write three note cards to describe the model
    C) make sure everyone does their own model
    D) listen to what another group is doing

3. Think about how the word *team* relates to *group*. Which words relate in the same way?

    team : group

    A) build : model
    B) role : job
    C) copy : original
    D) write : talk

4. The *focus* of the project is working as a team. Working as a team will be

    A) what they will do last
    B) how they will take a clear picture
    C) why they will have to make note cards
    D) the main activity

5. Which statement is true?

    A) Each person will fill a role.
    B) Each person will visit a different place.
    C) Each person will talk to the class.
    D) Each person will write three index cards.

Following Directions

Reminder from Mom

These are new words to practice.
Say each word 10 times.

* dentist
* appointment
* bagel
* counter

* remember
* office
* guard
* instructions

Choose one new word to write.

_____
- -
_____

Reminder from Mom

Story

Darcy,

Your dentist appointment is at 4:00 today.
I have to work late so Sherry's mom will drive you there. You may have a snack after school. There are bagels on the counter and there is juice in the refrigerator. Remember to brush your teeth after you eat.

The dentist will have your mouth guard ready. He will tell you how to take care of it. Listen to his instructions carefully.

You should walk over to Sherry's house at 3:30. I will pick you up at the dentist's office at 5:00. See you soon!

Love,
Mom

Darcy has a dentist appointment today. The next door neighbor will take Darcy to the dentist. Her daughter Sherry is Darcy's friend.

The dentist will give Darcy a mouth guard. The coach says Darcy has to wear it to play basketball. She should take good care of the mouth guard so it doesn't break. After the dentist sees Darcy, the hygienist will clean her teeth.

Darcy doesn't always enjoy going to the dentist. She would rather play after school. But she likes to have clean teeth!

Reminder from Mom

Quiz

Read the note and the story.

Use the note and the story to answer the questions.

1. Darcy will wear a mouth guard to play basketball. A mouth guard
   - Ⓐ will save her from an enemy
   - Ⓑ will protect her teeth
   - Ⓒ will make sure she doesn't talk
   - Ⓓ will make it easier to brush her teeth

2. This story is mainly about
   - Ⓐ a dentist appointment
   - Ⓑ a friend
   - Ⓒ a snack
   - Ⓓ a mouth guard

3. Who will take Darcy to the dentist?
   - Ⓐ Darcy's mother
   - Ⓑ Sherry's father
   - Ⓒ the next door neighbor
   - Ⓓ Darcy's aunt

4. What will Darcy do first when she gets home from school?
   - Ⓐ eat a snack
   - Ⓑ brush her teeth
   - Ⓒ walk to Sherry's house
   - Ⓓ listen carefully

5. Think about how the word *mouth* relates to the word *guard*. Which words relate in the same way?

   | mouth : guard |

   - Ⓐ walk : drive
   - Ⓑ listen : instructions
   - Ⓒ dentist : office
   - Ⓓ head : helmet

©Teacher Created Resources, Inc.   #8864 Informational Reading

Scout Camp

New Words

These are new words to practice.
Say each word 10 times.

- kitchen
- duty
- silverware
- soak
- wipe
- rinse
- rack
- flick

Choose one new word to write.

Scout Camp

Story

CAMP NEWS

Kitchen Duty

1. Fill plastic tubs with soapy water.
2. Put any cups, silverware, or other dishes in tubs to soak.
3. Throw away trash.
4. Wipe the tables.
5. Wash dishes.
6. Rinse dishes.
7. Set dishes on rack to dry.
8. Wash pots and pans.
9. Put away pots and pans.
10. Sweep floor.
11. Mop floor.

Brandon and Scott went to scout camp. The camp had tents, cabins, and a main hall. The main hall had tables, benches, a stage, and a kitchen.

On the second day of camp, Brandon and Scott had kitchen duty. It was their turn to help clean up the kitchen and dining area.

The scout leader posted a kitchen duty sign in the kitchen. It told the boys what to do to clean the kitchen.

Brandon read the sign and put soapy water in the plastic tubs. He flicked some of the water on Scott. Scott tossed the silverware in the tubs. He made sure a few soapsuds landed on Brandon. Scott took out the trash. Brandon wiped tables, flicking the rag on Scott as he finished each table. Brandon washed the dishes while Scott dried them. They washed all the pots and pans. Brandon swept the floor then Scott mopped it. Finally they were done with their job. They had fun doing kitchen duty.

©Teacher Created Resources, Inc. #8864 Informational Reading

Scout Camp

Quiz

Read the directions. Read the story.

Use the directions and the story to answer the questions.

1. Where did Scott put the silverware?

    (A) in a kitchen drawer
    (B) in the dishwasher
    (C) in a plastic tub with soapy water
    (D) on the tables in the main hall

2. The scouts ate

    (A) on the grass
    (B) in the cabins
    (C) by the lake
    (D) in the main hall

3. This story is mainly about

    (A) scout camp
    (B) kitchen duty
    (C) how to sweep the floor
    (D) taking out the trash

4. Think about how the word *wash* relates to the word *rinse*. Which words relate in the same way?

    wash : rinse

    (A) floor : table
    (B) sweep : mop
    (C) kitchen : duty
    (D) eat : dining

5. Brandon and Scott had kitchen duty. This means that they would

    (A) pay a tax
    (B) do something boring
    (C) earn a badge
    (D) do some work

#8864 Informational Reading   38   ©Teacher Created Resources, Inc.

Party Time

New Words

**These are new words to practice.
Say each word 10 times.**

- tablecloth
- streamer
- banner
- confetti
- honor
- award
- congratulate
- napkin

Choose one new word to write.

Party Time

Story

Set Up for the Party

- ☐ Put four chairs at each table.
- ☐ Put a tablecloth on each table. You will find tablecloths folded up on the side counter.
- ☐ Have a grownup help you hang streamers.
- ☐ Caleb will help blow up balloons.
- ☐ Holly can help you hang up the balloons. Fern, Holly, and Caleb will hang the banner.
- ☐ Place confetti in the center of each table.
- ☐ Set plates, cups, and napkins on the side counter.

Fern's school will get out for summer vacation next week. Her class will host a party. They will honor students who receive awards. They will congratulate those students.

Fern and some other students in her class will help set up for the party. Fern's teacher wrote her a list of things she will need to do while setting up. Fern will help put up decorations and set out the refreshments.

Everyone who attends the party will get to have cupcakes and juice. Fern and her friend Holly are very excited about the party. They like to have a good time with their friends.

Party Time

Quiz

Read the directions. Read the story.

Use the directions and the story to answer the questions.

1. Fern's class will *congratulate* some students. The class will
   - Ⓐ tell the students they will have a party
   - Ⓑ praise the students on their good work
   - Ⓒ be in a different class next year
   - Ⓓ wish the students good luck

2. This story is mainly about
   - Ⓐ having cake and juice
   - Ⓑ hanging streamers
   - Ⓒ setting up for a party
   - Ⓓ cleaning a room

3. The banner most likely says
   - Ⓐ congratulations
   - Ⓑ welcome
   - Ⓒ happy birthday
   - Ⓓ happy new year

4. What will Holly and Fern do with the balloons?
   - Ⓐ pop them
   - Ⓑ play with them
   - Ⓒ blow them up
   - Ⓓ hang them up

5. Think about how the word *balloons* relates to the word *decorations*. Which words relate in the same way?

   | balloons : decorations |

   - Ⓐ table : chairs
   - Ⓑ party : award
   - Ⓒ cupcakes : refreshments
   - Ⓓ confetti : streamers

©Teacher Created Resources, Inc.   41   #8864 Informational Reading

State Report

New Words

These are new words to practice.
Say each word 10 times.

- subject
- assignment
- title
- indent
- paragraph
- handwritten
- font
- review

Choose one new word to write.

State Report

Story

```
Subject:                                    Name:

Assignment:                                 Date:
```

Title

   Indent paragraphs. For handwritten papers you should skip lines. If you type the paper use double space. On the computer use Times New Roman 12 point font. For papers more than one page long, number the pages in the top right corner.

Kaylee has to do a report on her state for a class assignment. Her teacher gave the class this assignment sheet. It gives instructions on how to turn in the final report.

The teacher reviewed the instructions with the students. The subject of this report is social studies. Kaylee will write "state report" as the title of her assignment.

Kaylee will read books about her state and take notes. She might also visit places of interest or interview people to get more information.

Kaylee will carefully type her final report. She will follow all of her teacher's instructions. Kaylee will work hard to do a good job on this assignment.

State Report

Quiz

Read the directions. Read the story.

Use the directions and the story to answer the questions.

1. In the top left corner Kaylee should write

    Ⓐ her name
    Ⓑ the date
    Ⓒ the subject
    Ⓓ the title

2. Kaylee's report will most likely be about

    Ⓐ the state in which a historical event took place
    Ⓑ the state in which she lives
    Ⓒ the state she would like to visit
    Ⓓ the state with the most people

3. This story is mainly about

    Ⓐ how to write your name
    Ⓑ how to type on a computer
    Ⓒ how to indent a paragraph
    Ⓓ how to write a report

4. Think about how the word *type* relates to the word *computer*. Which words relate in the same way?

    type : computer

    Ⓐ write : pencil
    Ⓑ subject : assignment
    Ⓒ social studies : math
    Ⓓ review : report

5. Kaylee should *indent* each new paragraph. She will start writing

    Ⓐ at the red line on the paper
    Ⓑ in the center of a line
    Ⓒ at the top of the page
    Ⓓ a few spaces in from the left margin

#8864 Informational Reading ©Teacher Created Resources, Inc.

First Day

New Words

These are new words to practice.
Say each word 10 times.

- boulevard
- neighborhood
- avenue
- distance
- traffic light
- sketches
- crosswalk
- directions

Choose one new word to write.

_____

- -

_____

First Day

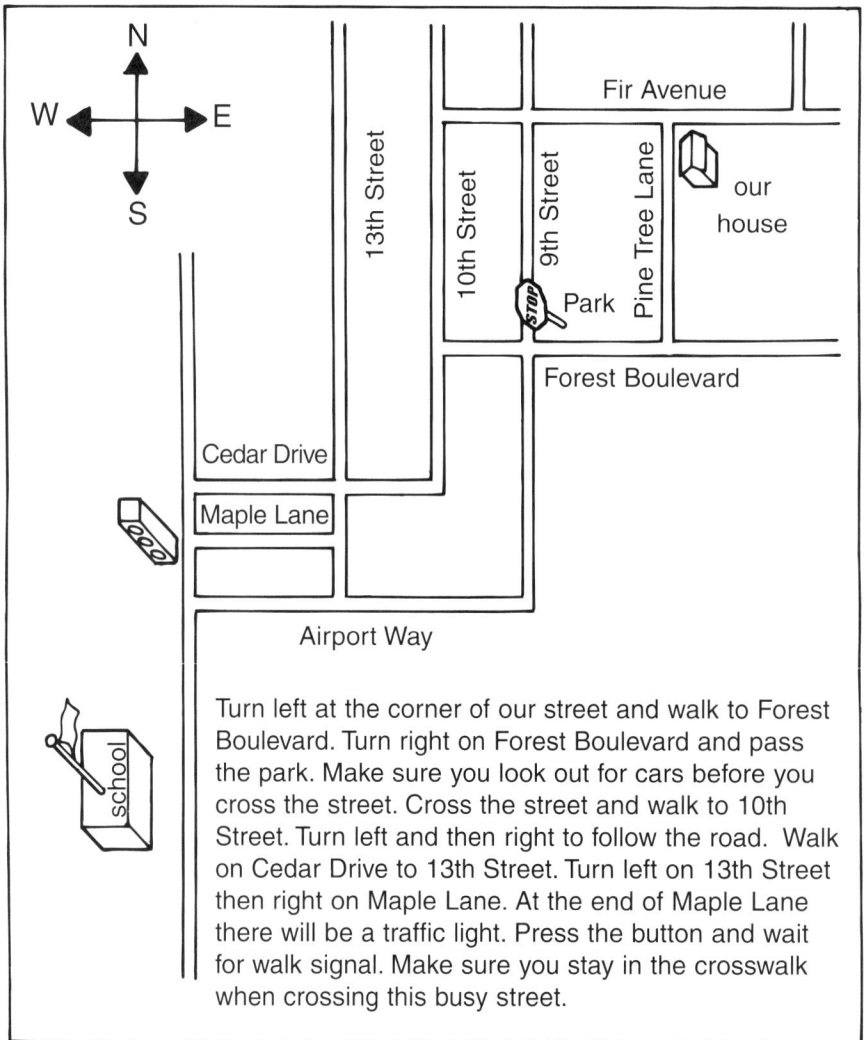

Turn left at the corner of our street and walk to Forest Boulevard. Turn right on Forest Boulevard and pass the park. Make sure you look out for cars before you cross the street. Cross the street and walk to 10th Street. Turn left and then right to follow the road. Walk on Cedar Drive to 13th Street. Turn left on 13th Street then right on Maple Lane. At the end of Maple Lane there will be a traffic light. Press the button and wait for walk signal. Make sure you stay in the crosswalk when crossing this busy street.

Adam just moved to a new neighborhood. Today will be his first day at a new school. The school he will attend is within walking distance of his house.

Adam wants to walk to school by himself this year. He needs directions so his mother finds a picture of the neighborhood. The picture shows the location of Adam's house and the school. His mother types in the street names he will use to get to school.

Adam's mother writes detailed directions for Adam. The directions tell him when to turn left and when to turn right. They also tell him to be careful as he walks. Adam will read the directions and look at the map to find his way to school.

First Day

Quiz

Read the directions. Read the story.

Use the directions and the story to answer the questions.

1. This story is mainly about
   - Ⓐ crossing the street
   - Ⓑ reading directions
   - Ⓒ drawing a picture
   - Ⓓ going to a new school

2. Adam lives on Fir Avenue. He lives
   - Ⓐ by many trees
   - Ⓑ near a park
   - Ⓒ next to school
   - Ⓓ by a highway

3. Think about how the word *street* relates to the word *road*. Which words relate in the same way?

   | street : road |

   - Ⓐ walk : run
   - Ⓑ stop : sign
   - Ⓒ lane : drive
   - Ⓓ trees : park

4. Adam will cross the street
   - Ⓐ on a bicycle
   - Ⓑ in the crosswalk
   - Ⓒ in a car
   - Ⓓ after he gets to school

5. Why does Adam need directions to get to school?
   - Ⓐ He moved to a new neighborhood.
   - Ⓑ He cannot read street signs.
   - Ⓒ He will attend two schools.
   - Ⓓ He will get lost

Build a Kite

New Words

**These are new words to practice.
Say each word 10 times.**

- materials
- pole
- diameter
- spool

- procedure
- slit
- thread
- diagram

Choose one new word to write.

_____

- -

_____

Build a Kite

Story

Sled Kite

Materials:

one black garbage bag

two 3' round poles, 1/8" diameter

spool of kite string

four 4" pieces of tape

one swivel hook

Procedure:

1. Cut 6 slits in the bag as shown.
2. Place poles inside the bag. Push them to the sides of the bag.
3. Cut 4 4" pieces of tape.
4. Tape the poles in place through the slits.
5. Cut 2 square holes in the middle of the bag as shown.
6. Cut 2 pieces of string, each about 2' long.
7. Thread a piece of string through the center slit by each pole. Tie the string to the pole.
8. Tie the ends of the string together with a swivel hook at the end.
9. Connect the hook to the spool of kite string. Fly!

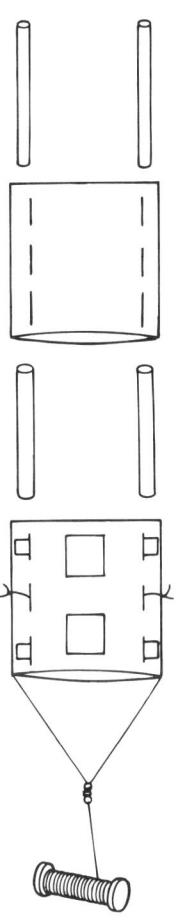

Nathan's dad collects different kinds of kites. He taught Nathan how to build a kite called a sled. It is made from a large black plastic trash bag.

Nathan's dad gave him a sheet of directions that explained the steps to build the kite. The directions also had diagrams that showed how to put the kite together.

When Nathan began to make the kite, he carefully laid the garbage bag out flat. He measured, evenly spaced, and cut six slits near the side edges of the bag. He inserted the poles into the bag and he taped them in place. He cut the square holes for air vents. Finally, he attached the string. After he was finished, he took his kite out for its first flight.

Build a Kite

Quiz

Read the directions. Read the story.

Use the directions and the story to answer the questions.

1. What is the length of each pole?

    A) one foot
    B) two feet
    C) three feet
    D) eight feet

2. Which statement is not true?

    A) The kite is made from a garbage bag.
    B) The kite is made of special paper.
    C) The kite did not fly.
    D) The poles are round.

3. This story is mainly about

    A) making a kite
    B) two poles
    C) a garbage bag
    D) a boy and his dad

4. Think about how the word *kite* relates to the word *fly*. Which words relate in the same way?

    kite : fly

    A) inches : feet
    B) ball : round
    C) tape : string
    D) boat : sail

5. Nathan cut a *slit* in the garbage bag. He cut

    A) a small hole
    B) a slice of melon
    C) the bag into pieces
    D) a long narrow opening

Pancake Breakfast

New Words

**These are new words to practice.
Say each word 10 times.**

- buttermilk
- sift
- liquid
- blend
- ingredients
- griddle
- batter
- recipe

Choose one new word to write.

_____

- -

_____

Pancake Breakfast

Story

Pancakes

Stir together:

1 egg

2 Tablespoons oil

1 ¼ cup buttermilk

Sift together:

1 ¼ cup flour

1 teaspoon sugar

1 teaspoon baking powder

½ teaspoon baking soda

½ teaspoon salt

Stir into liquid. Stir to blend all ingredients.

Heat 1 Tablespoon oil on griddle at 350°. Use a spoon to pour batter on pan to make a pancake.

Ben wanted to surprise his mother and make breakfast for her. He decided to cook pancakes.

Ben found an easy pancake recipe. His older sister helped him get out ingredients. She got the griddle and plugged it in.

Ben read the recipe and mixed the liquid ingredients in a large bowl. He added the dry ingredients and sifted them together. His sister helped him pour the batter on the griddle.

Ben cooked the pancakes until they were golden brown. He served them with melted butter and syrup. He brought the pancakes to his mother. She enjoyed her surprise.

Pancake Breakfast

Quiz

Read the recipe. Read the story.

Use the recipe and the story to answer the questions.

1. Ben cooked the pancakes on a *griddle*. He used
   - Ⓐ a barbecue
   - Ⓑ a large flat pan with a handle
   - Ⓒ a long fork
   - Ⓓ a microwave

2. This story is mainly about
   - Ⓐ how to eat breakfast
   - Ⓑ how to crack an egg
   - Ⓒ how to make pancakes
   - Ⓓ how to turn on the griddle

3. The recipe calls for the same amount of which two ingredients?
   - Ⓐ eggs and oil
   - Ⓑ sugar and baking powder
   - Ⓒ flour and salt
   - Ⓓ buttermilk and eggs

4. Which ingredients did Ben mix first?
   - Ⓐ ingredients that are sweet
   - Ⓑ ingredients that are dry
   - Ⓒ ingredients that are liquid
   - Ⓓ ingredients that are salty

5. Think about how the word *pour* relates to the word *buttermilk*. Which words relate in the same way?

   | pour : buttermilk |

   - Ⓐ sift : flour
   - Ⓑ teaspoon : tablespoon
   - Ⓒ sugar : salt
   - Ⓓ blend : mix

Crazy Hair

New Words

These are new words to practice.
Say each word 10 times.

- apply
- lather
- thoroughly
- repeat

- desire
- condition
- curly
- dye

Choose one new word to write.

Crazy Hair

Story

Directions:

Apply to wet hair.

Lather.

Rinse thoroughly.

Repeat if desired.

For best results comb hair while still wet.

Tame your wild hair!

Conditioning shampoo for dry or curly hair

Keri's mom helped Keri dye her hair. Keri's school had "crazy hair day" today. Keri colored her hair green with temporary hair dye. Tomorrow at school, Keri's hair must be back to its normal color.

Keri has curly hair and the dye made her hair frizzy. Keri wants to tame and smooth her hair. She also needs to wash all of the dye out of her hair.

Her mother gave her some special shampoo. Keri read the directions to find out if it will smooth her hair and wash out the green color.

Crazy Hair

Quiz

Look at the picture. Read the story.

Use the picture and the story to answer the questions.

1. This story is mainly about
   - Ⓐ a fun day at school
   - Ⓑ Keri's hair
   - Ⓒ Mom's advice
   - Ⓓ a special conditioning shampoo

2. Why will Keri rinse her hair?
   - Ⓐ to make it a different color
   - Ⓑ to get the soap out
   - Ⓒ to make it curly
   - Ⓓ to get her hair dry

3. Think about how the word *wet* relates to the word *dry*. Which words relate in the same way?

   wet : dry

   - Ⓐ lather : rinse
   - Ⓑ shampoo : soap
   - Ⓒ curly : straight
   - Ⓓ comb : brush

4. Keri should comb her hair
   - Ⓐ while it is still wet
   - Ⓑ every day
   - Ⓒ when she remembers
   - Ⓓ when it is dry

5. When Keri *applies* the shampoo
   - Ⓐ she will put it on the counter
   - Ⓑ she will put it on her hand
   - Ⓒ she will put it on her hair
   - Ⓓ she will paint it on her head

#8864 Informational Reading ©Teacher Created Resources, Inc.

Adopt a Pet

New Words

**These are new words to practice.
Say each word 10 times.**

* species
* breed
* retriever
* allergic

* flea
* rabies
* pound
* volunteer

Choose one new word to write.

_____

- - - - - - - - - - - - - - -

_____

Adopt a Pet

Story

Puddy

Area: northwest

Age: 1 year 3 months

Species: dog

Breed: retriever

Color: red and white

Eyes: brown

Sex: male

Received: 7/12/07

Comment: owner allergic

Puddy has had one flea treatment. He needs a rabies shot and license.

Johan's family wanted to get a pet. They went to the pound to look at the animals up for adoption. Johan's sister looked at cats. Johan and his father went to the dog section.

Johan found several dogs to choose from. His father liked what he read about a dog named Puddy. He asked a volunteer if the family could spend some time with Puddy out in the yard. They took Puddy outside to play with him. Johan and his sister really liked Puddy.

Johan's father filled out papers to adopt Puddy. The volunteer told him to take the dog to the vet for a shot. They will also need to get a collar and leash for their new pet.

Adopt a Pet

Quiz

**Read the information card. Read the story.
Use the information and the story to answer the questions.**

1. Puddy's previous owner was *allergic* to dogs. He

    Ⓐ got a cold
    Ⓑ sneezed and itched
    Ⓒ had many dogs at his house
    Ⓓ liked to adopt dogs

2. What breed of dog is Puddy?

    Ⓐ poodle
    Ⓑ collie
    Ⓒ retriever
    Ⓓ basset hound

3. This story is mainly about

    Ⓐ adopting a pet
    Ⓑ getting a shot
    Ⓒ finding a cat
    Ⓓ feeding a dog

4. Why is Puddy at the pound?

    Ⓐ He has a serious disease.
    Ⓑ He ran away from home.
    Ⓒ His previous owner is allergic to dogs.
    Ⓓ He doesn't like cats.

5. Think about how the word *red* relates to the word *color*. Which words relate in the same way?

    | **red : color** |

    Ⓐ male : dog
    Ⓑ fleas : rabies
    Ⓒ collar : leash
    Ⓓ dog : animal

Stay Healthy

New Words

These are new words to practice.
Say each word 10 times.

- inform
- virus
- potential
- symptom
- risk
- fatigue
- respiratory
- utensil

Choose one new word to write.

Story

Stay Healthy

Dear Parent:

We need to inform you of a potential health risk. A virus has been going around. Many students have been exposed to this virus. It affects the respiratory system.

Common symptoms include sneezing and a runny nose. A child may also have a fever and fatigue.

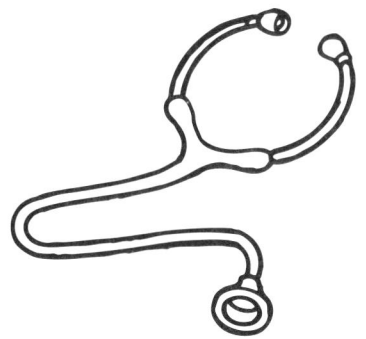

If your child has any of these symptoms, please keep him home from school. Students may return to school when they have not shown any symptoms for 24 hours.

Help your child reduce her risk of illness. Have her wash her hands often. Remind your child to wash them before and after meals and after using the restroom.

Students should not share food or any eating utensils. They should not share items of clothing.

We wish you and your children a healthy school year. Thank you for following these health guidelines.

Sincerely,

Kathy Nolan

School Nurse

One day Hanna brought this note home from school. She showed it to her mother. Hanna told her mother that many of her friends had missed school because they were sick.

Hanna and her mother talked about the letter. Her mother asked Hanna how many days of school her friends had missed. She wanted to know how long the virus usually lasts. Hanna said her friends were absent about two or three days.

Hanna's mother reminded her to wash her hands often. She told Hanna not to trade food at lunch. Hanna promised to try to stay healthy.

Stay Healthy

Quiz

Read the letter. Read the story.

Use the letter and the story to answer the questions.

1. What is one thing students can do to stay healthy?

    Ⓐ wear a coat
    Ⓑ stay home from school
    Ⓒ watch the teacher
    Ⓓ wash their hands often

2. This story is mainly about

    Ⓐ how to call the nurse
    Ⓑ how to stay healthy
    Ⓒ how to sneeze
    Ⓓ how to return to school

3. What is a tiny particle that causes disease?

    Ⓐ a cold
    Ⓑ an illness
    Ⓒ a virus
    Ⓓ a symptom

4. Think about how the word *ill* relates to the word *healthy*. Which words relate in the same way?

    ill : healthy

    Ⓐ fever : symptom
    Ⓑ sick : well
    Ⓒ wash : hands
    Ⓓ home : school

5. What are two of the symptoms of this virus?

    Ⓐ fever and fatigue
    Ⓑ cough and fever
    Ⓒ headache and runny nose
    Ⓓ sneezing and coughing

Getting Ready for Fall

New Words

**These are new words to practice.
Say each word 10 times.**

- weed
- gather
- cucumber
- pickle
- prepare
- almond
- rake
- meat

Choose one new word to write.

_____

- -

_____

Getting Ready for Fall

Story

FALL YARD CHORES

Weed the flower beds.
- Don't pull the flowers.
- Do pull the weeds.
- Ask if you are not sure if something is a weed or a flower.

Gather dead leaves and plants from the garden into a pile.

Pick cucumbers.

Help make pickles.

Weed garden: pumpkin, corn, and tomatoes

Prepare fall garden.

Plant fall garden: lettuce and peas

Pick up trash before dad mows.

Pick up any early walnuts from the grass.

Pick up after dog.

Rake leaves.

Kenyon's dad made a detailed list of chores that need to be done in the yard. He makes a new list for each season. Kenyon thinks some of the chores are difficult, but he will try to do his best.

Kenyon helps weed his mom's flower bed. He is learning the difference between weeds and plants and flowers. He also helps weed the garden.

The summer garden has been mostly harvested. Kenyon will help gather dead plants into a pile. Kenyon's dad always plants a few vegetables that grow quickly in the cooler weather. They can eat these vegetables before winter.

A large walnut tree stands just at the edge of the lawn. Kenyon must pick up walnut hulls before his dad can mow. Later Kenyon will help crack walnuts. He will pick out the nut meats.

He will also have to rake up the leaves before his dad mows the lawn. Before he rakes, he will have to pick up after the dog.

Getting Ready for Fall

Quiz

Read the list. Read the story.

Use the list and the story to answer the questions.

1. This story is mainly about
   - Ⓐ making pickles
   - Ⓑ eating walnuts
   - Ⓒ working in the yard
   - Ⓓ gathering dead plants

2. Kenyon will eat nut *meats* later this fall. He will eat
   - Ⓐ fruit that grows on a tree
   - Ⓑ the hull of the nut
   - Ⓒ part of an animal
   - Ⓓ the edible part of the nut

3. Think about how the word *vegetable* relates to the word *garden*. Which words relate in the same way?

   | **vegetable : garden** |

   - Ⓐ flower : bed
   - Ⓑ summer : fall
   - Ⓒ cucumber : pumpkin
   - Ⓓ rake : leaves

4. Which statement is not true?
   - Ⓐ The walnut tree stands at the edge of the lawn.
   - Ⓑ The summer garden has been harvested.
   - Ⓒ Kenyon's dad plants vegetables for a winter garden.
   - Ⓓ Kenyon has to pick up walnut hulls.

5. What will Kenyon's dad plant in the fall garden?
   - Ⓐ cucumber and pumpkin
   - Ⓑ peas and lettuce
   - Ⓒ lettuce and tomato
   - Ⓓ corn and peas

©Teacher Created Resources, Inc.   65   #8864 Informational Reading

Movie Time

New Words

These are new words to practice.
Say each word 10 times.

- volume
- audio
- video
- previous
- next
- scan
- pause
- menu

Choose one new word to write.

_____
- -
_____

Movie Time

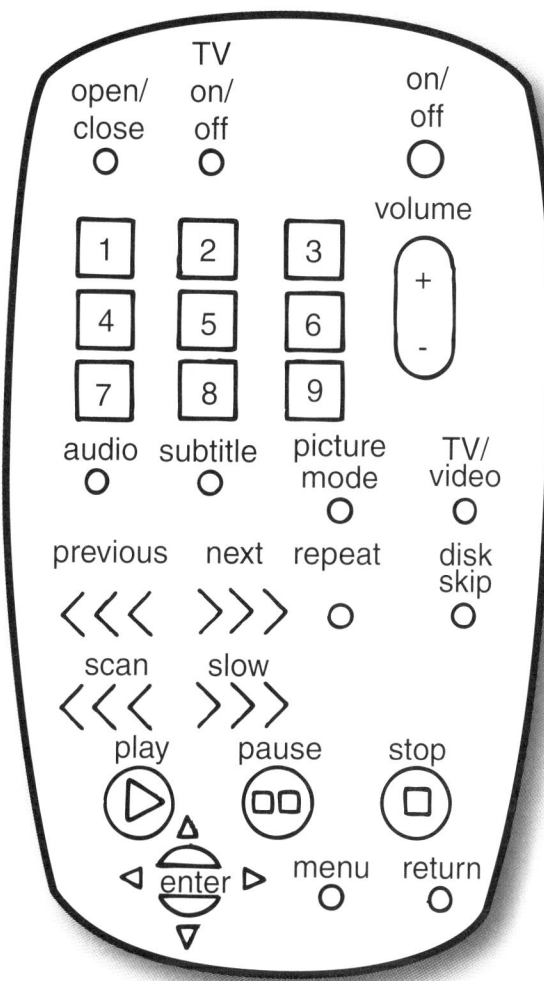

Tonight Ryan is having a friend over to spend the night. They want to watch a movie. They decided to watch "The Last Voyage to Earth," a science fiction movie.

Ryan knows how to operate the DVD player. He finds the remote control in the stereo cabinet. Ryan gets the DVD from the shelf.

Ryan presses the on/off button to turn on the machine. He presses the open/close button on the remote control. He puts the disk in the DVD player.

Next Ryan turns on the TV. He selects video on the remote control. He presses the play button.

After awhile, Ryan and Carlos get thirsty. They pause the DVD and get a snack. They start the movie again. Ryan wants to replay the scene they saw just before they paused the movie. He presses previous. They finish watching the movie while they are enjoying their snack.

Movie Time

Quiz

Look at the picture. Read the story.

Use the picture and the story to answer the questions.

1. Which button would Ryan push to put a DVD in the machine?

    Ⓐ open/close
    Ⓑ volume
    Ⓒ disk skip
    Ⓓ play

2. Why did Ryan press previous?

    Ⓐ to make the sound louder
    Ⓑ to watch a scene again
    Ⓒ to put in a different DVD
    Ⓓ to turn off the DVD player

3. This story is mainly about

    Ⓐ playing a game
    Ⓑ watching a DVD
    Ⓒ listening to music
    Ⓓ pushing a button

4. If Ryan *pauses* the DVD, he

    Ⓐ stops it for a short time
    Ⓑ pokes holes in the box
    Ⓒ turns it off
    Ⓓ plays it again

5. Think about how the word *previous* relates to the word *next*. Which words relate in the same way?

    previous : next

    Ⓐ repeat : return
    Ⓑ audio : video
    Ⓒ play : movie
    Ⓓ open : close

Summer Plans

New Words

These are new words to practice.
Say each word 10 times.

* visit
* campground
* far
* couple
* extra
* toast
* receive
* address

Choose one new word to write.

Summer Plans

Dear Ginny,

Guess what? My mom told me that our family will go camping in two weeks. We will stay at the campground by the river that's close to your house. Can you stay with us for a couple days? We have extra room in our tent but you'll have to bring your own sleeping bag. I'll be so excited if you can come! I hope your parents say okay.

We can toast marshmallows and make s'mores with chocolate, graham crackers, and marshmallows. We can also build a fort out of branches and leaves by the river. Maybe my dad will take us to the lake to go fishing. I'm not very good at catching fish but its fun to try. We'll have to stand on shore and hope we can find a deep place with fish.

Please call me when you receive this letter. You won't have enough time before we leave to mail a letter back. I hope you can come!

Your friend,

Rachel

Ginny went to the mailbox to get the mail. She saw a letter addressed to her. It was from her friend Rachel. Rachel used to live in the same town as Ginny, but she moved away. Rachel and her family will be camping close to Ginny's house.

Ginny enjoyed reading the letter. She couldn't wait to talk to her parents. She hoped her parents would let her go camping. She wanted to see Rachel again. She wanted to make a fort together. Ginny's favorite part of camping is having campfires. She also likes to sleep outside.

Summer Plans

Quiz

Read the letter. Read the story.

Use the letter and the story to answer the questions.

1. When people *camp*, they
   - A stay in one place
   - B live outside for awhile in a tent
   - C go to a place with many activities
   - D stay in a big building with a pool

2. This story is mainly about
   - A moving away
   - B a sleeping bag
   - C going on a camping trip
   - D building a fort

3. Where will Rachel and Ginny mostly likely toast marshmallows?
   - A in a toaster
   - B on a barbecue
   - C in an oven
   - D over a fire

4. Think about how the word *river* relates to the word *lake*. Which words relate in the same way?

   | river : lake |

   - A campground : house
   - B toast : roast
   - C stream : pond
   - D tent : sleeping bag

5. Where will Rachel's family camp?
   - A by the river
   - B at Ginny's house
   - C in a trailer
   - D by the ocean

©Teacher Created Resources, Inc.   71   #8864 Informational Reading

Winter Holiday Concert

New Words

**These are new words to practice.
Say each word 10 times.**

* concert
* harmony
* welcome
* band

* chorus
* choir
* intermission
* conductor

Choose one new word to write.

Winter Holiday Concert

Story

**Holiday Harmonies
Willow Creek School
Winter Concert**
Thursday, December 13
6:30 – 8:00 P.M.

Welcome	Mr. Harris, Principal
Flag Salute	Cub Scout Pack 668
Primary Rhythm Band	Miss Williams, Conductor
Fourth Grade Recorder Class	Mr. Sorsby, Conductor
Fourth Grade Chorus	Miss Williams, Director
Intermission	
Intermediate Band	Mr. Sorsby, Conductor
Fifth & Sixth Grade Choir	Miss Williams, Director
Closing	

*Thank you for coming to tonight's performance.
Refreshments will be served following the concert.*

Fonda's school had a winter concert. Everyone who attended received this program. It lists each music group and when they will perform.

Thursday afternoon everyone in the concert met in the gym. They had a final practice. Miss Williams and Mr. Sorsby told each group where to stand. The practice went well. Everyone was ready for the concert.

Fonda played the recorder with her class. They played two songs. Next year she will sing in the choir. Fonda loves to sing and play music.

Winter Holiday Concert

Quiz

Read the program. Read the story.

Use the program and the story to answer the questions.

1. What happens immediately after Fonda's recorder class performs?

    A) intermission
    B) primary rhythm band
    C) fourth grade chorus
    D) flag salute

2. Fonda plays a *recorder*. She plays

    A) a musical instrument like a flute
    B) a machine that puts sounds on a tape or disk
    C) better than anyone else
    D) a tool that writes facts

3. This story is mainly about

    A) a group of people
    B) a winter concert
    C) a flute
    D) a band

4. What day of the week did the concert take place?

    A) Thursday
    B) Tuesday
    C) Monday
    D) Wednesday

5. Think about how the word *concert* relates to the word *performance*. Which words relate in the same way?

    concert : performance

    A) band : choir
    B) conductor : singer
    C) welcome : closing
    D) recorder : flute

#8864 Informational Reading © Teacher Created Resources, Inc.

Gymnastics Class

New Words

These are new words to practice.
Say each word 10 times.

* medal
* gym
* gymnastics
* tumbling

* balance
* introduction
* skill
* acrobatics

Choose one new word to write.

_____

- -

_____

Gymnastics Class

GOLD MEDAL GYM

Gymnastics Classes for all ages

$4.00/session
$40.00/class for 12 sessions

TUMBLING TOTS Monday, Wednesday, Friday
age 3-5 years 9:30-10:30 A.M.
large motor skill development
children learn basic tumbling moves on floor mats

BEGINNING BALANCE Tuesday, Thursday
age 6-8 years 3:30-5:00 P.M.
introduction to balance beam, springboard, and bar

JUNIOR GYMNASTS Monday, Wednesday, Friday
age 9-11 years 3:00-4:30 P.M.
tumbling and gymnastics skills

ACROBATICS FOR CHEERLEADERS Tuesday, Thursday
age 12-14 years 2:30-4:00 P.M.
advanced tumbling and acrobatics
learn to incorporate dance moves to create a routine

Last summer Jen watched the Olympics on TV. Her favorite sport to watch was gymnastics. She enjoyed watching the floor routines. Jen's mom said she should take gymnastics lessons. Jen thought that was a great idea.

The first season, Jen's mom signed her up for Junior Gymnasts. Jen was going to learn tumbling skills. She wanted to learn to do a back handspring.

Jen wanted to learn to use more of the equipment so this season she worked on the parallel bars. The teacher introduced the pommel horse. Jen worked on the balance beam again and learned to do a somersault on it.

Gymnastics is Jen's favorite sport. Perhaps some day she can try out for a team.

Gymnastics Class

Quiz

Read the schedule. Read the story.

Use the schedule and the story to answer the questions.

1. How did Jen first find out about gymnastics?

    Ⓐ She watched the Olympics.
    Ⓑ She went to the gym.
    Ⓒ She talked to a friend.
    Ⓓ She turned somersaults at home.

2. This strory is mainly about

    Ⓐ medals
    Ⓑ gymnastics
    Ⓒ bars
    Ⓓ cheerleaders

3. When Jen learned to *balance* well, she could

    Ⓐ carry two glasses at once
    Ⓑ ride in a hot air balloon
    Ⓒ keep steady and not fall over
    Ⓓ jump over a bar

4. Think about how the word *beginning* relates to the word *advanced*. Which words relate in the same way?

    > beginning : advanced

    Ⓐ acrobatics : gymnastics
    Ⓑ beam : bar
    Ⓒ tumbling : mat
    Ⓓ easy : difficult

5. Which days will Jen have gymnastics?

    Ⓐ Monday, Tuesday, Thursday
    Ⓑ Monday, Wednesday, Friday
    Ⓒ Monday, Wednesday
    Ⓓ Tuesday, Thursday

Visit a Volcano

New Words

These are new words to practice.
Say each word 10 times.

- volcano
- picnic
- departure
- schedule
- tour
- trail
- ridge
- arrive

Choose one new word to write.

_____

- - - - - - - - - - - - - - - - - - -

_____

Visit a Volcano

Story

MT. ST. HELENS FIELD TRIP

Depart from School	8:00 A.M.	
Silver Lake Visitor's Center	9:45–10:45	Tour
		Snack & bathroom
Coldwater Ridge Visitor's Center	11:45–12:45	Tour
Coldwater Lake Picnic Area	12:45–1:15	Lunch & bathroom
Johnston Ridge Visitor's Center	1:30–2:30	Tour
Hummock Trail	3:00–4:00	Hike the trail
Coldwater Lake Picnic Area	4:15–4:30	Bathroom
Kelso	6:15–7:00	Dinner
Arrive at School	8:00 P.M.	Go home

Reagan is in 5th grade. Every year the fifth grade classes take a field trip to Mt. St. Helens Volcano. Reagan's class went on the field trip with the other fifth grade classes.

It would take two hours to get to the volcanic monument area. The trip would take all day. They would arrive back at school after dinner. The fifth grade teachers planned the field trip. They gave a copy of the schedule to each student.

Reagan read the schedule carefully. He wanted to know which visitor centers the class would see. He showed the schedule to his parents. They were glad the classes would visit all three visitor centers.

Visit a Volcano

Quiz

Read the schedule. Read the story.

Use the schedule and the story to answer the questions.

1. Reagan's class hiked on a *trail* through hummocks. A trail is

   Ⓐ a treat made with mixed nuts
   Ⓑ a path or track
   Ⓒ a low rounded hill
   Ⓓ lava inside a volcano's crater

2. Why will the group stop in Kelso?

   Ⓐ to see a volcano
   Ⓑ to go to a gift shop
   Ⓒ to see a video
   Ⓓ to have dinner

3. This story is mainly about

   Ⓐ going on a field trip.
   Ⓑ watching a volcano erupt.
   Ⓒ swimming in a lake.
   Ⓓ staying out past dinner.

4. What will Reagan's class do after they tour Johnston Ridge?

   Ⓐ tour Silver Lake
   Ⓑ hike the Hummock Trail
   Ⓒ look at Coldwater Ridge
   Ⓓ have lunch

5. Think about how the word *depart* relates to the word *arrive*. Which words relate in the same way?

   depart : arrive

   Ⓐ hike : trail
   Ⓑ lunch : dinner
   Ⓒ begin : end
   Ⓓ ridge : mountain

Fair Days

New Words

**These are new words to practice.
Say each word 10 times.**

- ceremony
- arena
- midway
- exhibit
- livestock
- demonstration
- grandstand
- discount

Choose one new word to write.

Fair Days

Story

Date	Event	Time	Location
Friday August 3	Opening ceremonies	6:30 P.M.	Center courtyard
Saturday August 4	Livestock judging	10:00 A.M.	Livestock arena
	Earthshake Concert	7:00 P.M.	Grandstand
Sunday August 5	Livestock judging	11:00 A.M.	Livestock arena
	Photography exhibit opens	2:00 P.M.	Fine arts building
Monday August 6	4-H demonstrations	11:00 A.M.	4-H building
Tuesday August 7	Petting zoo	6:00 P.M.	Livestock arena
Wednesday August 8	Livestock judging	9:00 A.M.	Livestock arena
Thursday August 9	Jones & Grimm circus	6:00 P.M.	Grandstand
Friday August 10	Spiffy Soda Bracelet Day	1-5 P.M.	Midway
	Louis Krane Concert	7:00 P.M.	Grandstand
Saturday August 11	Kiddie Carnival	1:00 P.M.	Center courtyard
Sunday August 12	Monster truck race	2:00 P.M.	Grandstand

Tessa's family went to the fair. They went on Friday, August 10. Tessa's mother wanted to get the discount on rides.

Tessa's father wanted to hear the Louis Krane concert. Her brother Rob would rather go on Sunday because he wanted to see the monster truck race.

Tessa loves the fair. She didn't care when they went.

They got to the fair in the morning. Tessa wanted to see the sheep. She likes to look at the goats. She wanted to look at flower exhibits. Her mother wanted to see the quilts.

They got hungry after looking at all the exhibits. Tessa's family went to the food barn. They had hot dogs and lemonade for lunch.

Tessa's mother said they could have a snack later. They could have caramel corn or ice cream.

Tessa's mother bought two bracelets at a booth on their way to the rides. Rob and Tessa could each go on rides. They used "Spiffy Soda" coupons and got a discount on the price.

After Rob and Tessa rode their favorite rides they were hot, dusty, and tired. They got cold ice cream for their dessert. The ice cream sure tasted good!

Fair Days

Quiz

Look at the schedule. Read the story.

Use the schedule and the story to answer the questions.

1. Where will Rob go to look at photographs?

    Ⓐ home economics building
    Ⓑ livestock arena
    Ⓒ fine arts building
    Ⓓ central courtyard

2. This story is mainly about

    Ⓐ raising sheep
    Ⓑ going to the fair
    Ⓒ eating an ice cream cone
    Ⓓ riding a roller coaster

3. Which statement is true?

    Ⓐ Tessa could see the circus.
    Ⓑ Tessa could see the petting zoo.
    Ⓒ Tessa could go on an amusement ride.
    Ⓓ Tessa could watch a cooking demonstration.

4. What could Tessa's family see at the grandstand on Friday?

    Ⓐ Louis Crane concert
    Ⓑ Monster Truck race
    Ⓒ Jones & Grimm circus
    Ⓓ Earthshake concert

5. Think about how the word *sheep* relates to the word *animal*. Which words relate in the same way?

    sheep : animal

    Ⓐ cake : candy
    Ⓑ monster : truck
    Ⓒ carnival : midway
    Ⓓ cows : livestock

Friday Night at the Movies

New Words

**These are new words to practice.
Say each word 10 times.**

✻ cinema	✻ matinee
✻ theater	✻ apply
✻ voyage	✻ coupon
✻ lens	✻ accept

Choose one new word to write.

_____

- -

_____

Friday Night at the Movies

Story

Friday, November 9

Cinemas 4 216 SE Cherry Ln				
Sam, the Small Horse	12:40	2:40	4:40	6:40
Riduculi	1:00	3:00	5:00	7:00
Upside Down Twins	1:30	3:30	5:30	7:30
Voyage to the Frozen Zone	1:50	3:50	5:50	7:50
Royal Theaters **2413 Main St.**				
Riduculi	1:00	3:00	5:00	7:00
Lens	1:20	3:20	5:20	7:20
A Cat Called Kiki	1:30	3:30	5:30	7:30
Voyage to the Frozen Zone	1:50	3:50	5:50	7:50
Woodfellows	2:00	4:00	6:00	8:00
Matinee prices apply to showings before 5:00 P.M. *No coupons accepted on Friday and Saturday*				

Jose wants to go to the movie theatre. He finds the newspaper and reads the movie listings. He wants to see a science fiction or adventure movie. Jose asks his friend Travis if he wants to see the movie with him. They talk about which movie to watch. Travis doesn't think Voyage to the Frozen Zone sounds too interesting. They decide to go see Lens instead.

Both boys want to save money. They go to the matinee show at 3:20 P.M. They pay less for their tickets. By saving money they can go to movies more often. Jose enjoys watching movies at the theater.

Friday Night at the Movies

Quiz

Look at the schedule. Read the story.

Use the schedule and the story to answer the questions.

1. This story is mainly about
   - Ⓐ movie listings
   - Ⓑ theater coupons
   - Ⓒ friendship
   - Ⓓ matinee prices

2. Jose and Travis will attend a *matinee*. They will see a movie
   - Ⓐ in the morning
   - Ⓑ on a Sunday
   - Ⓒ in the afternoon
   - Ⓓ in the evening

3. Which movie is showing at both theaters?
   - Ⓐ Upside Down Twins
   - Ⓑ Lens
   - Ⓒ Sam, the Small Horse
   - Ⓓ Voyage to the Frozen Zone

4. Think about how the word *cinema* relates to the word *theater*. Which words relate in the same way?

   > **cinema : theater**

   - Ⓐ coupon : discount
   - Ⓑ movie : listing
   - Ⓒ voyage : journey
   - Ⓓ cat : horse

5. What will the theater not take on Friday night?
   - Ⓐ snacks
   - Ⓑ coupons
   - Ⓒ tickets
   - Ⓓ money

Computer Fun

New Words

**These are new words to practice.
Say each word 10 times.**

- education
- entertainment
- click
- product
- fact
- information
- Website
- original

Choose one new word to write.

_____
- -
_____

Computer Fun

Story

THE PLACE FOR EDUCATIONAL ENTERTAINMENT FOR ALL AGES

- About us
- Games
- Puzzles
- Coloring pages
- Fun Facts

RAINBOW CRAYONS

Click here to see our new products

New Sparkling Drinks for kids!

The sparkle, fizz, and taste you want.

Now in new flavors

No added sugars, so moms like them too!

Cherry, Orange, Strawberry

Kids! Find fun facts

Post a new and interesting bit of information on our web site. Each month we will choose a winning fact. Winners based on originality, creativity, and interest. Winners receive a CD with more games, facts, and activities to play on your computer.

Post Fact Now ☐

Read facts others have posted ☐

Amaze your friends with your knowledge!

Heather turns on her computer and connects to the Internet. She has a favorite Website that she often visits. It is a Website especially for kids. It has games and other fun activities.

Heather always checks the fun facts posted by other kids. Each month she posts a new fact she has found. She hopes one month her fun fact will be chosen as the winning fact. Heather likes to read the facts other kids have posted. It is fun to surprise her family and friends with an unusual bit of information.

Today Heather decides to look at the coloring pages. She prints out a beach scene that she will color. Heather enjoys her time on the Internet.

Computer Fun

Quiz

Look at the picture. Read the story.

Use the picture and the story to answer the questions.

1. The page has an advertisement for which product?

    Ⓐ markers
    Ⓑ crayons
    Ⓒ colored pencils
    Ⓓ watercolor paints

2. This story is mainly about

    Ⓐ reading a new fact
    Ⓑ printing a coloring page
    Ⓒ a place for kids to play
    Ⓓ a Website designed for kids

3. Think about how the word *information* relates to the word *fact*. Which words relate in the same way?

    > information : fact

    Ⓐ Website : Internet
    Ⓑ puzzle : game
    Ⓒ education : knowledge
    Ⓓ cherry : orange

4. What can Heather do if she wants to play a game?

    Ⓐ click on the link that says "games"
    Ⓑ go to a different Website
    Ⓒ turn off the computer
    Ⓓ click on the link that says "fun facts"

5. Why does Heather post new facts?

    Ⓐ She wants to try the new drinks.
    Ⓑ She wants to surprise her friends.
    Ⓒ She wants people to think she is smart.
    Ⓓ She wants to win a CD.

Four Wheeling

New Words

**These are new words to practice.
Say each word 10 times.**

* gear
* fatal
* injury
* suffocate

* essay
* feature
* heading
* italic

Choose one new word to write.

Four Wheeling

Story

by Lucas Sundby

Safety

When you go four wheeling you will need to wear *safety gear*. The most important item you'll need is a helmet. It is the only gear that is required by the law. Your head is in the most danger of receiving a *fatal* injury.

The chest plate is also very important because it helps protect you from being suffocated during a wreck. Wear proper pants so your legs won't get bruised or cut up too badly. Wear special boots so you don't break your ankles. Wear special gloves so you do not crush or break your hand. Last, you need the kill switch on your quad. You need this in case you fall off. It will shut off the quad in case of an emergency.

Dangers

Quad riding is very dangerous because if you flip you can get *suffocated*. If you flip the quad can roll over you. That's why you wear the proper gear. Without gear you can get serious injuries that may lead to death.

Benefits

Quad riding can be very fun when safety rules are followed. You can go off jumps and sometimes do tricks. You can enter races and win *trophies*. Sometimes the trophies are so big they can be bigger than a table. Quad riding is an exciting sport!

Students in Jason's class wrote essays. The teacher, Mr. Green, gave everyone a copy of this essay. It describes a particular sport.

This essay has some features of nonfiction text. Mr. Green explained those things.

He pointed out the title. He read the headings. He showed the class the words in italics. Those words are new vocabulary words.

Mr. Green put the class into groups. Jason's group read the essay and talked about it. They took turns finding the features of nonfiction text. They practiced reading many types of nonfiction texts.

Four Wheeling

Quiz

Read the essay. Read the story.

Use the essay and the story to answer the questions.

1. This story is mainly about
   - Ⓐ wearing safety gear
   - Ⓑ how to win a trophy
   - Ⓒ reading nonfiction text
   - Ⓓ how to ride a quad

2. Mr. Green explained nonfiction text features. He told about
   - Ⓐ the latest movies
   - Ⓑ the important parts and characteristics
   - Ⓒ the pictures on the page
   - Ⓓ the parts of a person's face

3. Which of these is a heading from the essay?
   - Ⓐ gear
   - Ⓑ jumps
   - Ⓒ dangers
   - Ⓓ trophies

4. How can Jason tell a word is a new vocabulary word?
   - Ⓐ It will be in blue ink.
   - Ⓑ It will be underlined.
   - Ⓒ It will be in capital letters.
   - Ⓓ It will be in italics.

5. Think about how the word *helmet* relates to the word *head*. Which words relate in the same way?

   helmet : head

   - Ⓐ gloves : hand
   - Ⓑ injury : hurt
   - Ⓒ danger : benefit
   - Ⓓ jumps : tricks

A Modern Artist

New Words

**These are new words to practice.
Say each word 10 times.**

- artist
- canvas
- famous
- achieve
- devote
- design
- pursue
- librarian

Choose one new word to write.

A Modern Artist

Story

THOMAS C. WEST
1937 – 1980

Thomas C. West never became a famous artist. He devoted most of his adult life to pursuing his passion for art.

Mr. West painted on canvas. He used oil and acrylic paints. He often attached scraps of canvas fabric to the main canvas surface. This achieved a three dimensional effect. He painted the picture over the canvas scraps.

Mr. West also worked with clay. He made pottery using a wheel. He made pitchers, cups, vases, and bowls.

Later in life, Thomas West designed swimming pools. He drew pictures that showed how the pool would be built. They showed exactly how the pool would look. He also designed the area surrounding the pool.

Dee's teacher gave an assignment. All students were required to read a biography. While reading the biography, Dee would learn about a person.

Dee's favorite subject is art so she chose to read about an artist.

Dee went to the school library and found this article in a newspaper. She read the article and took notes. She will write a one page report about the artist she studied.

Dee asked the librarian a question. She asked if the library had other books about Mr. West. The librarian said no. The librarian said that she knows a college professor who might have more information. The professor knew Mr. West.

It sounded fun to talk to a teacher at the college who knew Mr. West. Dee would get more information about his life. This would help her with her report.

Dee learned that Mr. West did many interesting things during his life. Dee had fun gathering many interesting facts about Mr. West.

A Modern Artist

Quiz

Read the biography. Read the story.

Use the biography and the story to answer the questions.

1. Mr. West was never *famous*. That means he was not

   A) living in a big house
   B) on television
   C) wealthy
   D) well known to many people.

2. What type of paint did Thomas West use?

   A) oils and acrylics
   B) watercolor
   C) finger paint
   D) poster paint

3. This story is mainly about

   A) a swimming pool
   B) an artist
   C) a painting
   D) a famous person

4. Think about how the word *canvas* relates to the word *fabric*. Which words relate in the same way?

   canvas : fabric

   A) swimming : pool
   B) design : draw
   C) acrylic : paint
   D) cup : bowl

5. How did Dee get more information after she read the biography?

   A) She asked the librarian for a video.
   B) She talked to someone who knew Mr. West.
   C) She read another book about Mr. West.
   D) She looked on the Internet.

©Teacher Created Resources, Inc.   95   #8864 Informational Reading

Technology in the News

New Words

**These are new words to practice.
Say each word 10 times.**

* technology
* model
* invent
* sponsor

* develop
* improve
* issue
* article

Choose one new word to write.

Technology in the News

Story

Scientists create new technology each year. Things we use every day are improved with new features. New products replace old ones. The new models are faster or better.

Here is an example of how this works. The first cell phones were large and awkward. The next year they were a bit smaller and easier to use.

Now cell phones are very light and come with many features. People can send text messages, listen to music, and take pictures.

Students can take part in the process of improving technology. They can invent new products and develop new ideas.

Some companies sponsor student contests. The contests look for new ideas and products.

Students can design something that uses technology and enter the contest.

Perhaps you have an idea. You may want to make your favorite product better. Who knows, it may become next year's hot new technology!

Each week Grant receives a newspaper at school. The class has to read the cover story. The cover story is the paper's main article. This issue has an article about technology. It tells how students can help develop and improve technology.

Grant wants to improve the light bulb. He thinks that light bulbs break too easily. Grant thinks that light bulbs should not be made of glass and should not break.

Grant reads the article. He wants to read more about technology so he saves the paper. He wants to read the article again to figure out how he will enter his idea in the contest.

Technology in the News

Quiz

Read the article. Read the story.

Use the article and the story to answer the questions.

1. Where did Grant read the technology article?

   Ⓐ in a book
   Ⓑ in a newspaper
   Ⓒ on the Internet
   Ⓓ in a magazine

2. This story is mainly about

   Ⓐ a new cell phone
   Ⓑ a technology contest
   Ⓒ a news article
   Ⓓ a glass light bulb

3. Why did Grant save the newspaper?

   Ⓐ He wanted to learn more about cell phones.
   Ⓑ He wanted to get a cell phone.
   Ⓒ He wanted to make a new invention.
   Ⓓ He wanted to enter the contest.

4. The article says scientists *develop* new technology. This means

   Ⓐ they build on technology we already have
   Ⓑ they grow plants
   Ⓒ they put chemicals on things
   Ⓓ they use old inventions

5. Think about how the word *large* relates to the word *small*. Which words relate in the same way?

   | large : small |

   Ⓐ new : old
   Ⓑ newspaper : article
   Ⓒ model : product
   Ⓓ invent : create

Anthology of Folk Tales

New Words

These are new words to practice.
Say each word 10 times.

- ✶ index
- ✶ anthology
- ✶ folk tale
- ✶ table of contents
- ✶ tall tale
- ✶ topics
- ✶ fable
- ✶ alphabetical

Choose one new word to write.

Anthology of Folk Tales

Story

Index

Folk Tales

Adventures of Spider, The (Africa)	6
Brer Rabbit and Tar Baby (United States)	19
Cinderella (France)	23
Dick Whittington and his Cat (Great Britain)	28
Hansel and Gretel (Germany)	35
Once a Mouse (India)	48
Puss in Boots (France)	65
Shoemaker and the Elves, The (Germany)	71
Steadfast Tin Soldier, The (Denmark)	78
Strega Nona (Italy)	85
Three Billy Goats Gruff (Norway)	98

Tall Tales

Mike Fink	40
Pecos Bill	60
Paul Bunyan	54

Fables

Boy Who Cried Wolf, The	15
Fox and the Grapes, The	33
Monkey and the Crocodile, The	44
Tortoise and the Hare, The	105
Ugly Duckling, The	111

Martin's class read folk tales this week. Mrs. Vonn brought in copies of an anthology. The students will read a selection of the folk tales in the anthology.

Mrs. Vonn showed the class the table of contents. She showed them illustrations. They also looked at the index at the back of the book.

Mrs. Vonn asked if anyone had seen an anthology before. Martin knew that an anthology is a collection of stories that are printed in one book.

She asked the students why they would use the index. Serena said an index is arranged in alphabetical order and she could easily find the item she wanted to read. The index shows the page number of each tale in the anthology.

Mrs. Vonn said that many other books have an index. Martin raised his hand. He knew that the science book has an index and that in the science book the index has a list of topics. It does not have titles of stories.

Anthology of Folk Tales

Quiz

Look at the index. Read the story.

Use the index and the story to answer the questions.

1. An alphabetical list that shows where to find things in a book is a(n)
   - Ⓐ glossary
   - Ⓑ dictionary
   - Ⓒ index
   - Ⓓ table of contents

2. What story will Martin find on page 65?
   - Ⓐ Puss in Boots
   - Ⓑ Strega Nona
   - Ⓒ Pecos Bill
   - Ⓓ Hansel and Gretel

3. This story is mainly about
   - Ⓐ reading a folk tale
   - Ⓑ using an index
   - Ⓒ writing words alphabetically
   - Ⓓ finding a topic

4. Think about how the word *tale* relates to the word *story*. Which words relate in the same way?

   tale : story

   - Ⓐ tortoise : hare
   - Ⓑ beginning : end
   - Ⓒ contents : index
   - Ⓓ anthology : collection

5. How is an index arranged?
   - Ⓐ by page number
   - Ⓑ by chapters
   - Ⓒ in alphabetical order
   - Ⓓ by topics of interest

Learning New Science Words

New Words

**These are new words to practice.
Say each word 10 times.**

- glossary
- distribute
- textbook
- familiar
- specific
- italic
- relate
- dictionary

Choose one new word to write.

_____

- - - - - - - - - - - - - - -

_____

Learning New Science Words

Glossary

algae – a tubeless plant

appendages – legs or other body parts

botanist – a scientist who studies plants

capture – to attract and hold

classify – to place into groups

conservation – protection of natural resources

crater – a large hole in the ground caused by a meteorite

current – movement of electricity through a wire

deciduous – trees that lose their leaves

defense – something that protects an animal from harm

density – the weight of an object compared to its size

gully – a ditch in the surface of the earth

incline – to lean or slant

inertia – resistance to an object's change in motion

luminous – giving off its own light

opaque – an object that light cannot pass through

pulley – a wheel with a groove around its outside

saliva – liquid in your mouth to keep it moist and help digest food

It is the beginning of a new school year. Mr. Hann distributed the science textbooks to each student in the class.

He asked the class to look at the book. He wanted them to get familiar with it.

Mr. Hann pointed out the glossary. The textbook has some words in italics.

If students do not know these words, they can look in the glossary. This glossary tells the meaning of science words.

Madi noticed the words are listed in alphabetical order. It looks similar to a dictionary. Mr. Hann said a glossary is smaller than a dictionary and easier to use.

A glossary is very specific. Madi may want to find out the meaning of a new word. If the word is not italicized then she would have to use the dictionary to find the meaning of the word.

Madi likes to learn. She enjoyed looking at the glossary. She thought she would use the glossary to help her find the meanings of unknown words. If she uses the glossary she will understand the words she is reading.

Learning New Science Words

Quiz

Look at the glossary. Read the story.

Use the glossary and the story to answer the questions.

1. What type of words does this glossary have?

    Ⓐ hi words
    Ⓑ science words
    Ⓒ math words
    Ⓓ English words

2. This story is mainly about

    Ⓐ using an index
    Ⓑ finding a dictionary
    Ⓒ using a glossary
    Ⓓ learning in a science class

3. Think about how the word *crater* relates to the word *hole*. Which words relate in the same way?

crater : hole

    Ⓐ gully : ditch
    Ⓑ teacher : student
    Ⓒ glossary : words
    Ⓓ alphabetical : order

4. What should Madi do if she cannot find a word in the glossary?

    Ⓐ ask a teacher
    Ⓑ look in a dictionary
    Ⓒ read the science textbook
    Ⓓ ignore it

5. The science book has a *glossary*. The *glossary*

    Ⓐ has a page with shiny pictures
    Ⓑ gives pages numbers for topics
    Ⓒ lists all the subjects in the science book
    Ⓓ explains the meaning of special terms used in the book

#8864 Informational Reading   104   ©Teacher Created Resources, Inc.

At the Lake

New Words

These are new words to practice.
Say each word 10 times.

- peninsula
- tennis
- amphitheater
- marina

- lifeguard
- launch
- recreation
- cousin

Choose one new word to write.

At the Lake

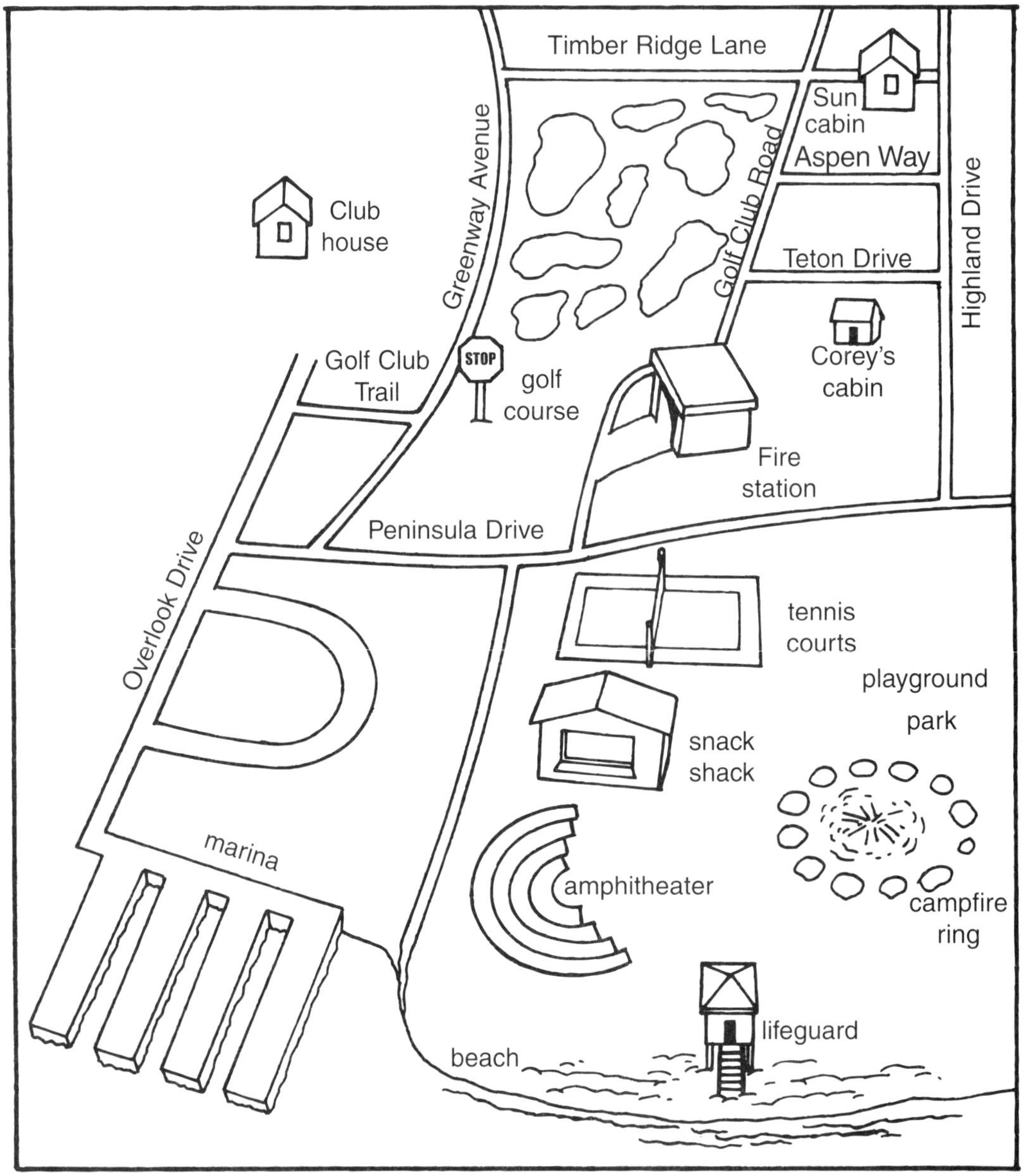

Story

Cole's cousin Hayley has a summer job at the lake. Hayley works for the recreation department of the country club located on the lake. Cole is staying at his grandmother's cabin on the lake and he will help Hayley work.

Tonight Cole will help Hayley with a kids' night at the park. They will show a movie at the amphitheater. After the movie some kids will play soccer or basketball.

Hayley's older cousins are also visiting. They live in another state. They are staying with Hayley's family at Sun cabin. They want to watch the movie. They will play at the park when the movie is over.

Hayley gave them a map that they will use to find the amphitheater. They will walk from the cabin to the park. Hayley marks the easiest route for them to take.

At the Lake

Quiz

Look at the map. Read the story.

Use the map and the story to answer the questions.

1. To get to the amphitheater, Hayley's cousins will walk past
   - Ⓐ the club house
   - Ⓑ the fire station
   - Ⓒ the marina
   - Ⓓ the beach

2. What could Hayley's cousins do at the beach?
   - Ⓐ roast marshmallows
   - Ⓑ get a snack
   - Ⓒ play golf
   - Ⓓ swim in the lake

3. This story is mainly about
   - Ⓐ Cole and Hayley working together
   - Ⓑ directions to the amphitheater
   - Ⓒ how to swim in the lake
   - Ⓓ how to get to the golf course

4. Hayley's job is in recreation. She helps people
   - Ⓐ play games or sports and do activities
   - Ⓑ make something new
   - Ⓒ launch a boat
   - Ⓓ fix a snack to eat

5. Think about how the word *boat* relates to *marina*. Which words relate in the same way?

   | **boat : marina** |

   - Ⓐ cabin : house
   - Ⓑ car : garage
   - Ⓒ lifeguard : beach
   - Ⓓ tennis : court

Exploring the Library

New Words

**These are new words to practice.
Say each word 10 times.**

- circulation
- adult
- catalog
- biography
- periodicals
- reference
- online
- pamphlet

Choose one new word to write.

_____

- -

_____

Exploring the Library

Story

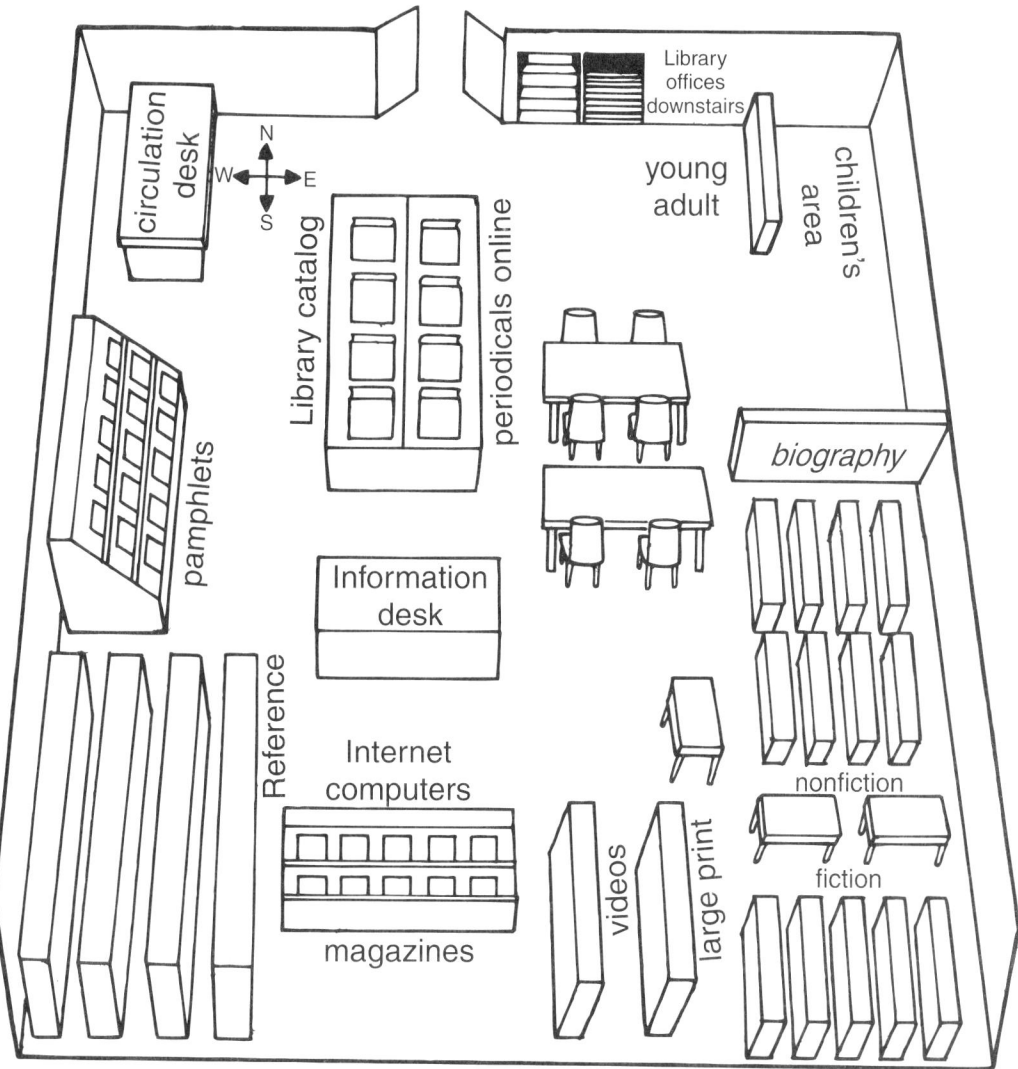

Amy went to the library with her mom. Her mom needed to go to the library to tutor a student.

Amy's mom picked up a map of the library. She gave the map to Amy. The map showed Amy where things in the library are located.

Amy's mom showed her the videos. She pointed to the library catalog. She told Amy where to find nonfiction. She showed Amy the magazines. She showed Amy the children's area.

Amy explored the library while her mom went to tutor the student. She looked up her favorite subjects in the catalog.

Amy found an art book in the catalog. She also found a book about computers. She went to the nonfiction section to get both books.

Amy wandered into the children's area. She picked out a book to read while she waited for her mom.

Exploring the Library

Quiz

Look at the map. Read the story.

Use the map and the story to answer the questions.

1. This story is mainly about
   - Ⓐ a computer
   - Ⓑ an information desk
   - Ⓒ a library
   - Ⓓ a movie

2. According to the map, where can Amy find children's books?
   - Ⓐ In the northeast corner of the library.
   - Ⓑ In the southeast corner of the library.
   - Ⓒ In the southwest corner of the library.
   - Ⓓ In the northwest corner of the library.

3. Think about how the word *fiction* relates to the word *nonfiction*. Which words relate in the same way?

   fiction : nonfiction

   - Ⓐ magazine : pages
   - Ⓑ shelves : catalog
   - Ⓒ library : books
   - Ⓓ child : adult

4. Amy used the library catalog to find a book. The catalog lists
   - Ⓐ Internet web sites
   - Ⓑ all the books in the library
   - Ⓒ places she could buy a book
   - Ⓓ pictures of people and objects

5. Why did Amy's mom give her a map?
   - Ⓐ to show Amy how to find the library
   - Ⓑ to show Amy how to read a book
   - Ⓒ to show Amy how to find things in the library
   - Ⓓ to show Amy how to check out a book

Shopping Day

New Words

**These are new words to practice.
Say each word 10 times.**

- shopping center
- mortgage
- drug store
- bagel
- haircut
- express
- agree
- medicine

Choose one new word to write.

Shopping Day

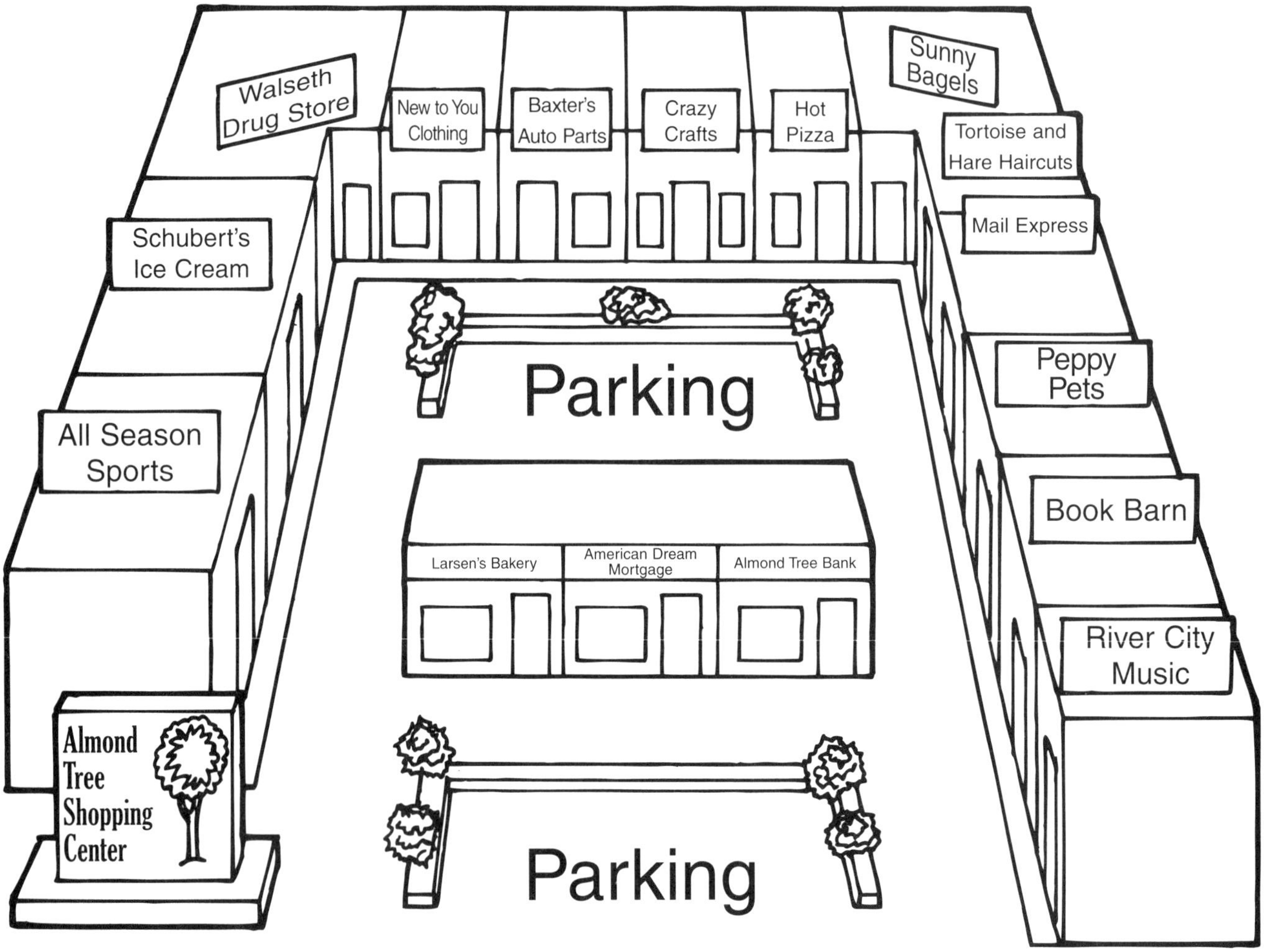

Story

Garrett had been saving his allowance for a few weeks. He wanted to go to the shopping center so he asked his mom to take him. His mom had some errands to do there so she agreed to take him.

Garrett didn't know what he wanted to buy so he decided to look around. The shopping center did not have a toy store. Garrett decided he'd look at the book store instead. He might also look at the CDs in the music store. As he walked by the pet store, he wondered if his mom would let him get a dog.

On the way home, Garrett's mother stopped at the bank. She deposited some money. She stopped by the drug store to pick up some toothpaste, shampoo, and allergy medicine.

Finally, they were on their way home. Garrett was disappointed because he did not find anything to buy.

Shopping Day

Quiz

Look at the map. Read the story.

Use the map and the story to answer the questions.

1. Why did Garrett's mother say yes when he asked to go to the shopping center?

    Ⓐ She wanted Garrett's money.
    Ⓑ She needed her car washed.
    Ⓒ She thought he told the truth.
    Ⓓ She needed to run errands there.

2. This story is mainly about

    Ⓐ a car wash
    Ⓑ a trip to the shopping center
    Ⓒ spending money
    Ⓓ mom's money

3. If Garrett wanted to buy a skateboard, in which store should he look?

    Ⓐ All Season Sports
    Ⓑ Baxter's Auto Parts
    Ⓒ Sunny Bagels
    Ⓓ New to You Resale Clothing Store

4. Which store is right next to the Book Barn?

    Ⓐ Crazy Crafts
    Ⓑ Larsen's Bakery
    Ⓒ River City Music
    Ⓓ Mail Express

5. Think about how the word *bagels* relates to the word *bread*. Which words relate in the same way?

    bagels : bread

    Ⓐ money : bank
    Ⓑ almond : nut
    Ⓒ shopping : center
    Ⓓ store : business

The World Around Us

New Words

**These are new words to practice.
Say each word 10 times.**

- environment
- protect
- wetland
- wildlife
- watershed
- recycle
- hazardous
- waste

Choose one new word to write.

_____

- -

_____

The World Around Us

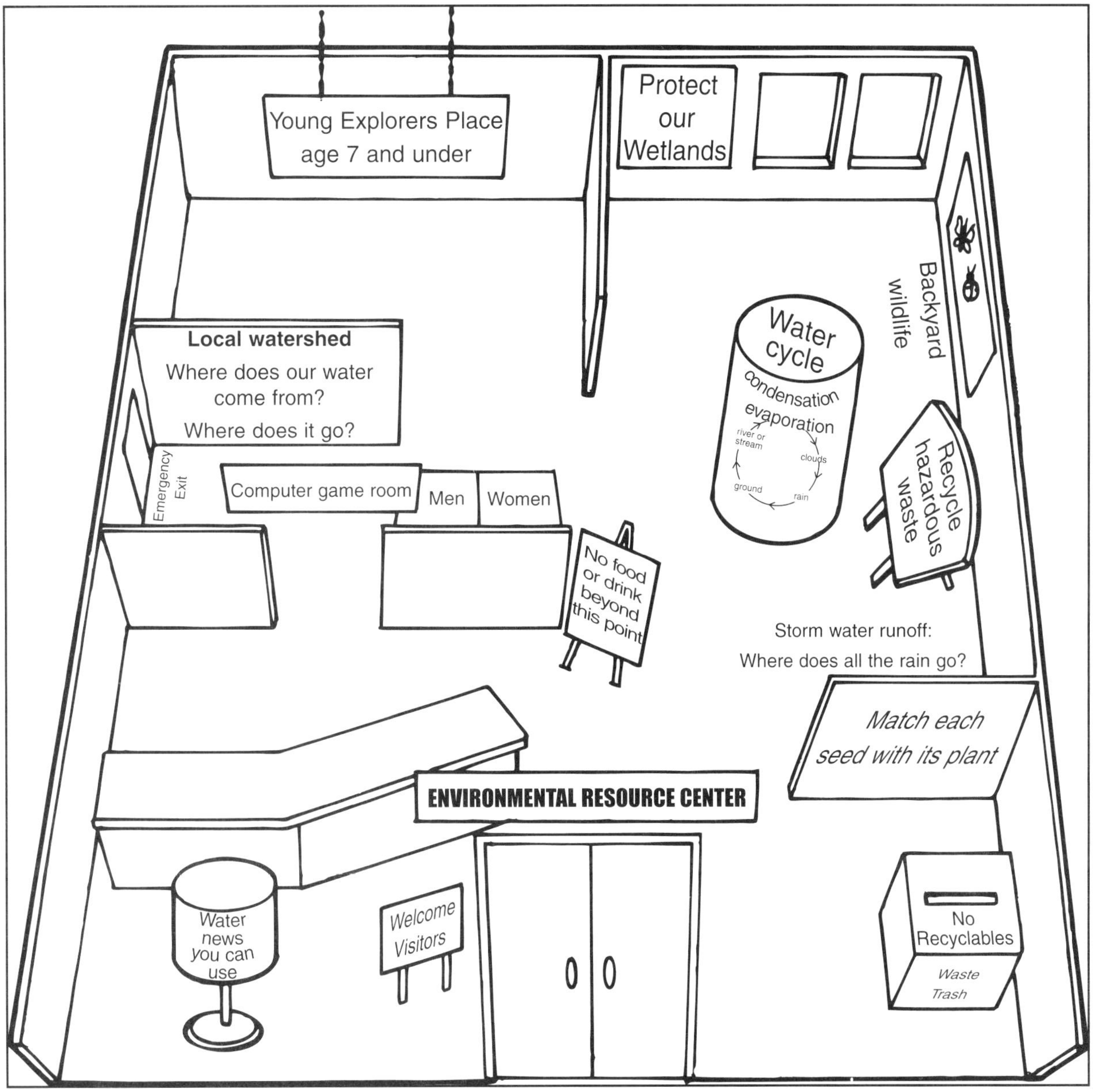

Story

Shawn's class went on a field trip to the environmental resource center.

His class has learned about many different plants and animals. They studied weather and the water cycle. In another week it will be Earth Day and they will discuss recycling.

A tour guide led the class through the resource center. She explained all the displays.

The guide talked with the students about recycling. Shawn felt proud that his family already recycles glass, paper, and plastic.

The class looked at a watershed map. It showed the rivers, streams, and lakes in their area. They also played the educational computer games. Shawn found the field trip very interesting.

The World Around Us

Quiz

Look at the map. Read the story.

Use the map and the story to answer the questions.

1. This story is mainly about

   Ⓐ recycling glass, paper, and plastic
   Ⓑ caring for seeds and plants
   Ⓒ becoming young explorers
   Ⓓ visiting an environmental center

2. The center has information about the *environment*. Shawn's *environment* consists of

   Ⓐ the things he recycles
   Ⓑ the things that affect his life
   Ⓒ the water he uses
   Ⓓ the animals in his backyard

3. Why should Shawn recycle hazardous waste?

   Ⓐ he can get money for recycling
   Ⓑ it won't fit in the garbage can
   Ⓒ it is dangerous material
   Ⓓ so it won't get in the water cycle

4. Think about how the word *rain* relates to the word *cloud*. Which words relate in the same way?

   rain : cloud

   Ⓐ come : go
   Ⓑ seed : plant
   Ⓒ waste : trash
   Ⓓ computer : game

5. Shawn could look at an exhibit on

   Ⓐ how to recycle
   Ⓑ how to watch the weather
   Ⓒ how to grow a garden
   Ⓓ how to drink water

#8864 Informational Reading 116 ©Teacher Created Resources, Inc.

Steven's New School

New Words

These are new words to practice.
Say each word 10 times.

* parking
* portable
* media
* resource

* talent
* gifted
* laboratory
* module

Choose one new word to write.

_____
- -
_____

Steven's New School

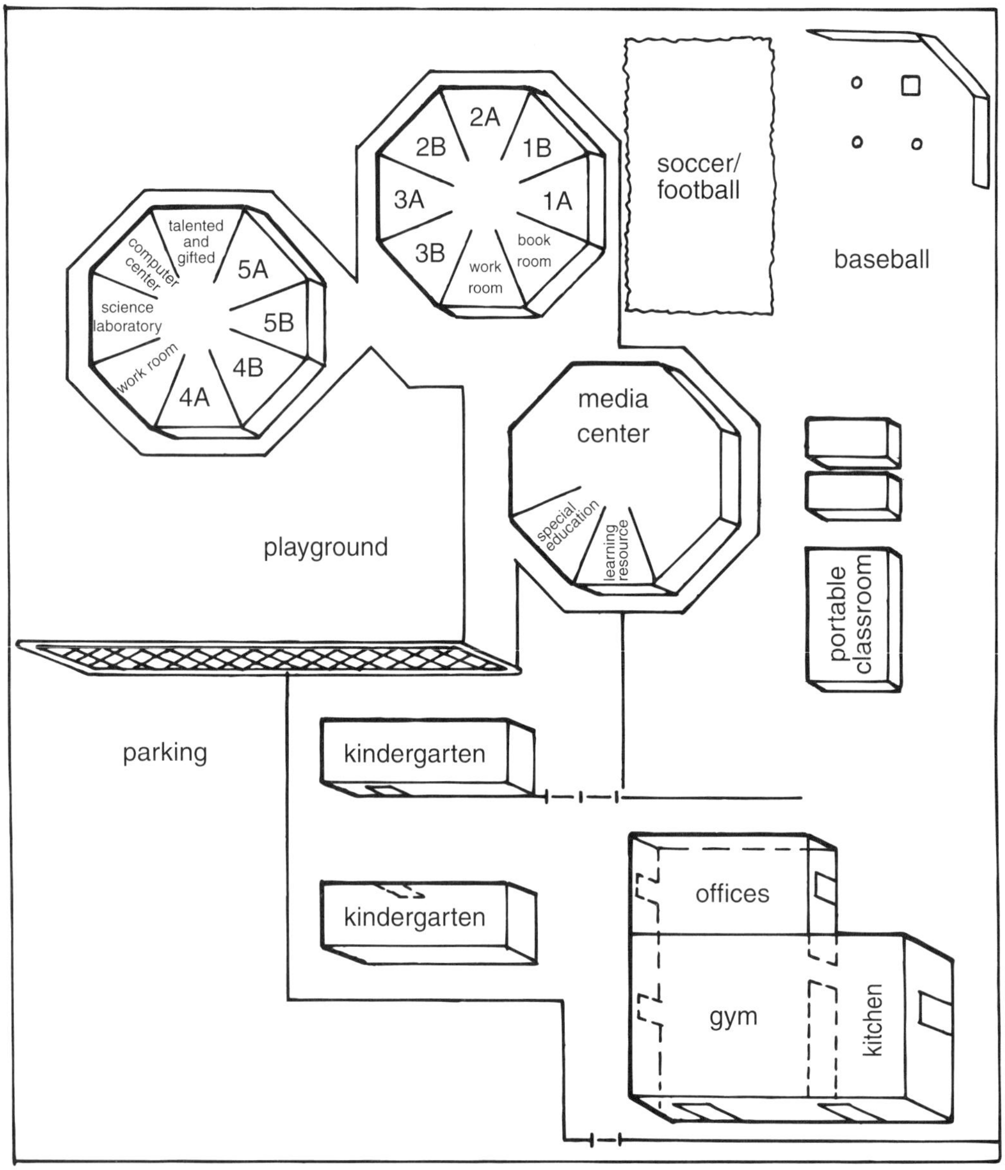

Maps

[Map of the school showing: modules containing rooms 2A, 2B, 1B, 3A, 1A, 3B, book room, work room; another module with talented and gifted, computer center, science laboratory, work room, 5A, 5B, 4B, 4A; soccer/football field; baseball field; media center with special education and learning resource; portable classroom; playground; parking; two kindergarten buildings; offices; gym; kitchen]

Steven and his family just moved to a new town. His parents took him to visit the school he will be attending. They registered Steven at his new school.

The secretary gave them a map. She explained that the school has modules connected by covered walkways.

Steven looked at the map with his parents. His classroom is room 4A. He will also go to the learning resource room to get extra help in math. Steven used the map and found the way from his classroom to the learning resource room.

Steven read the map carefully when he got home. He found the computer center on the map. He also found the science laboratory. He hoped his class would get to visit those rooms. Steven thought his new school might be fun.

#8864 Informational Reading   118   ©Teacher Created Resources, Inc.

Steven's New School

Quiz

Look at the map. Read the story.

Use the map and the story to answer the questions.

1. The school has *modules*. It has

   Ⓐ covered sidewalks

   Ⓑ easy and hard classes

   Ⓒ moving parts

   Ⓓ separate buildings linked together

2. This story is mainly about

   Ⓐ Learning in a science classroom

   Ⓑ looking at a map of a new school

   Ⓒ moving to a new place

   Ⓓ meeting a new student

3. Think about how the word *talented* relates to the word *gifted*. Which words relate in the same way?

talented : gifted

   Ⓐ module : space

   Ⓑ playground : swings

   Ⓒ media center : library

   Ⓓ parking : lot

4. Which other room is in the same module as learning resource?

   Ⓐ the computer center

   Ⓑ the science laboratory

   Ⓒ the media center

   Ⓓ the kitchen

5. Which statement is not true?

   Ⓐ Steven's classroom is next to room 3B.

   Ⓑ The book room is by the first grade classes.

   Ⓒ Learning resource is next to the media center.

   Ⓓ Steven's classroom is close to the playground.

©Teacher Created Resources, Inc.   119   #8864 Informational Reading

Sunday Bike Ride

New Words

These are new words to practice.
Say each word 10 times.

* route
* discovery
* pier
* legend

* overpass
* paved
* gravel
* posted

Choose one new word to write.

Sunday Bike Ride

Story

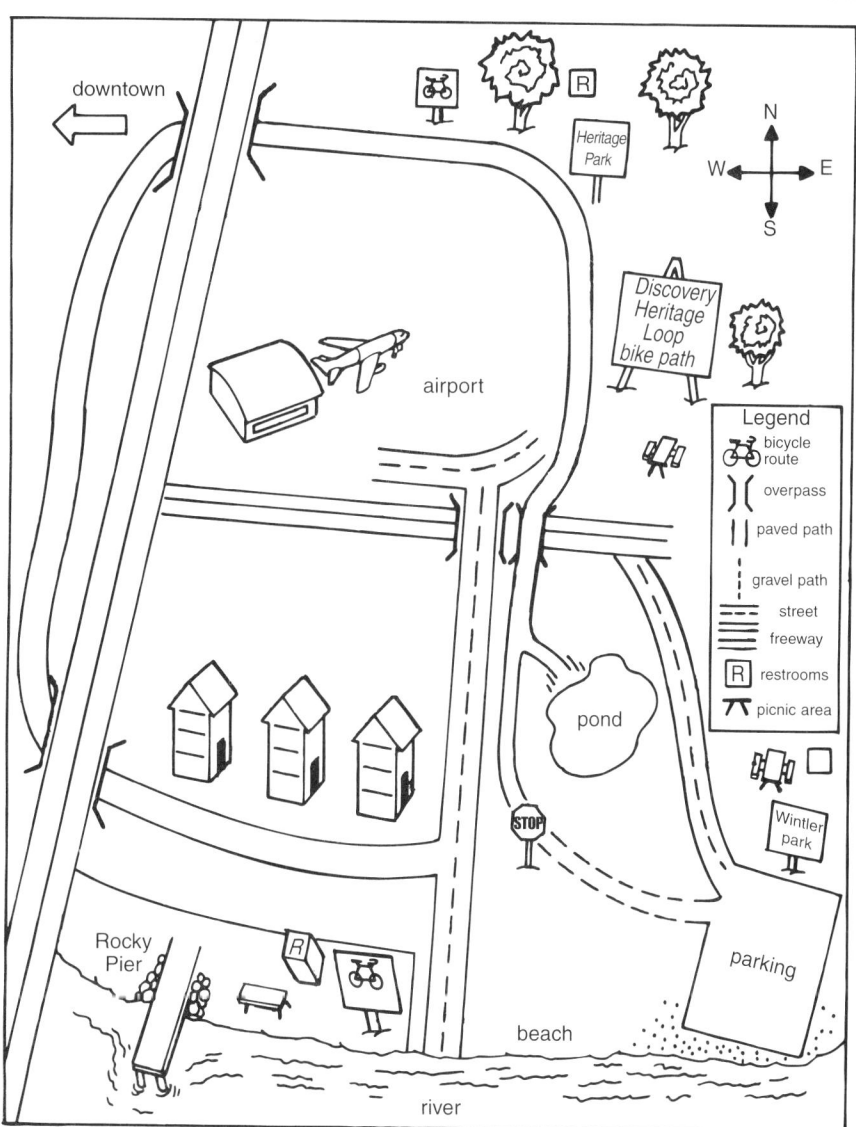

Juanita's family went on a bike ride with another family from their neighborhood. They went on Sunday afternoon.

They started at Heritage Park and rode to Wintler Park.

Juanita read the bike trail map that was posted at the park. She noticed that they would not travel the entire loop since they were not going to ride on the west side of the park. Juanita helped her family plan their route.

They rode south on the bike trail. They carefully crossed the overpass. At the stop sign they turned left on to the gravel path. The route went along the river. They also rode through a grassy area.

After their bike ride, the two families had a picnic. Juanita and her neighbors played on the beach. They waded in the river. Everyone rode their bikes back to Heritage Park.

©Teacher Created Resources, Inc. #8864 Informational Reading

Sunday Bike Ride

Quiz

Look at the map. Read the story.

Use the map and the story to answer the questions.

1. This story is mainly about
   - (A) playing on the beach
   - (B) having a picnic
   - (C) going on a bicycle ride
   - (D) seeing an airplane

2. What did Juanita see on her bike ride?
   - (A) an airport
   - (B) a train station
   - (C) Rocky Pier
   - (D) downtown

3. When Juanita rode on the overpass, what did she cross over?
   - (A) a gravel path
   - (B) a street
   - (C) the river
   - (D) the freeway

4. Think about how the word *path* relates to the word *route*. Which words relate in the same way?

   path : route

   - (A) gravel : paved
   - (B) overpass : bridge
   - (C) stop : sign
   - (D) pond : river

5. Part of the bike path is *gravel*. That part has
   - (A) lots of green grass
   - (B) tiny loose stones
   - (C) hard concrete
   - (D) rocks and tar

#8864 Informational Reading ©Teacher Created Resources, Inc.

Camp Woodleaf

New Words

**These are new words to practice.
Say each word 10 times.**

- meeting
- dining
- campfire
- activity

- archery
- range
- arrow
- message

Choose one new word to write.

Camp Woodleaf

Story

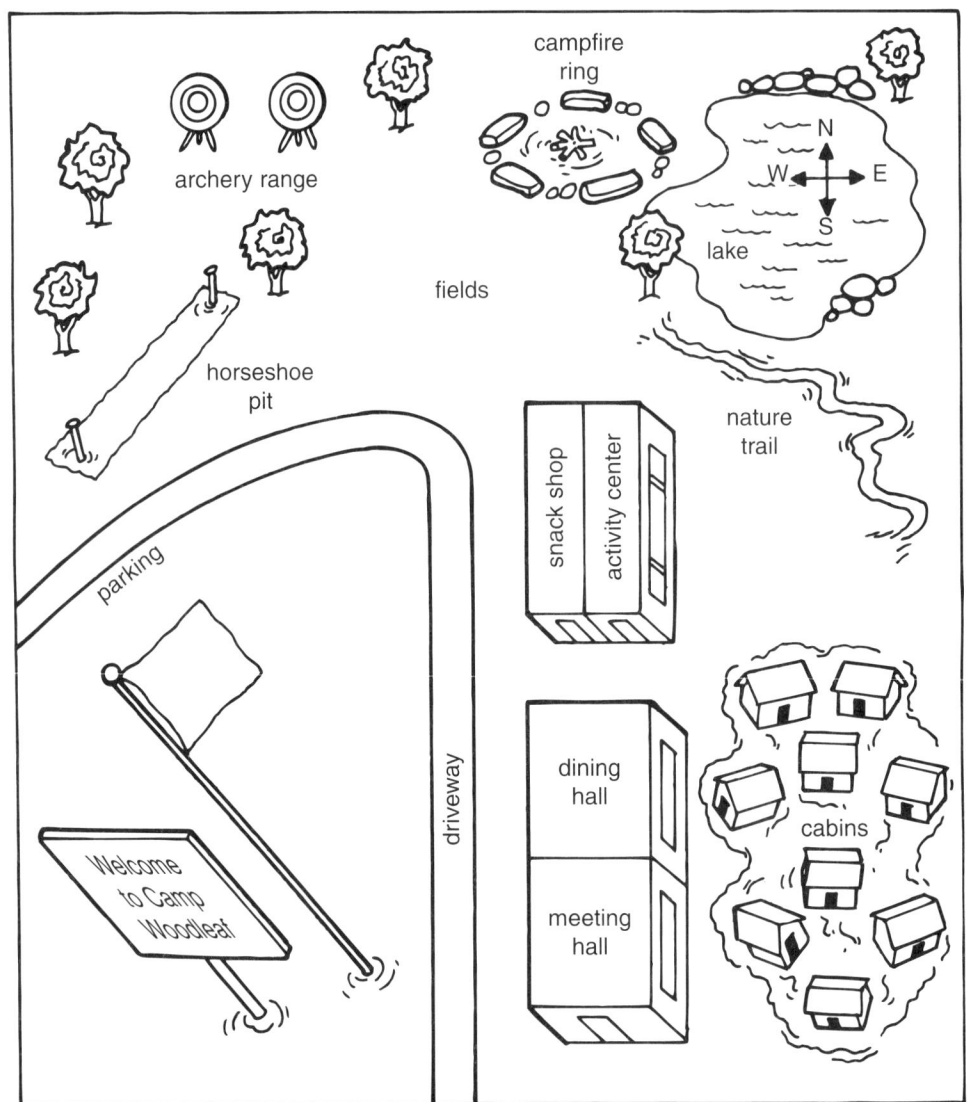

Today is Isaiah's first day of summer camp. He will stay at camp for seven days. When Isaiah gets to camp, the first thing he does is go to a camp meeting.

All the campers get together in a large meeting hall. They receive a map of the campground with the camp rules printed on the back.

One of the camp leaders assigns people to their cabins. A leader will post a schedule each day. He will put it on the message board on the wall outside the meeting hall. Campers are asked to read the schedule each day.

Isaiah looks at the map and finds the archery range. He would like to try shooting with a bow and arrow.

Isaiah also finds the lake and the nature trail. He plans to paddle a kayak on the lake, swim, and walk the trail. Isaiah sees the campfire ring. He loves sitting by campfires!

Camp Woodleaf

Quiz

Look at the map. Read the story.

Use the map and the story to answer the questions.

1. What is in the same building as the activity center?

   Ⓐ archery range
   Ⓑ snack shop
   Ⓒ campfire ring
   Ⓓ dining hall

2. Isaiah went to a *meeting*. It was

   Ⓐ a place to see new people
   Ⓑ a nature class
   Ⓒ an arranged time for people to get together to talk about camp
   Ⓓ a group of people playing games

3. This story is mainly about

   Ⓐ finding the way around camp
   Ⓑ having a campfire
   Ⓒ shooting arrows
   Ⓓ eating in the dining hall

4. Where can Isaiah go to get warm and roast marshmallows?

   Ⓐ the fields
   Ⓑ the horseshoe pit
   Ⓒ the campfire ring
   Ⓓ his cabin

5. Think about how the word *bow* relates to the word *arrow*. Which words relate in the same way?

   | **bow : arrow** |

   Ⓐ activity : center
   Ⓑ nature : walk
   Ⓒ snack : food
   Ⓓ kayak : paddles

©Teacher Created Resources, Inc.

Make a Hamburger

New Words

**These are new words to practice.
Say each word 10 times.**

- equipment
- deck
- complete
- common
- worth
- discard
- shuffle
- point

Choose one new word to write.

Make a Hamburger

Story

Card Game

Players: four

Object: Try to complete your hamburger with the most points before anyone else goes out of the game.

Equipment: deck of game cards

The deck of game cards has common items for a hamburger. There are four cards for each item, each with a picture. Each item is worth points, as indicated:

burger(3)   bun(2)   mayonnaise(1)
cheese(2)   bacon(1) mustard(1)
lettuce(3) tomato(2) ketchup(1)
pickle(1)   onion(1)

A complete hamburger must have both a bun and a burger. The more items you have, the more points you receive.

How to play:

Deal two cards to each person. Place the remainder of the deck face down. Players take turns drawing one card at a time. A player may discard one card if desired.

Lay down a completed hamburger any time after you have the bun and the burger. Try to get more items to get more points. You may only lay down a hamburger on your turn. Try to guess when the other players might have a completed hamburger.

Once someone has placed a complete hamburger on the table, that hand is over. That person counts up the total number of points showing on his cards.

All other players must lay down a bun and burger, if they can. They subtract the points for any other items they hold in their hand.

Tanner plays his new card game with his friends Jordan, Cole, and Evan. Tanner explains how to play the game. He shuffles the cards and deals. Cole plays first. After drawing a card, he has a bun, lettuce, and onion in his hand.

Jordan already has a bun and a burger in his hand. He wants more cards so he can get more points. He draws a pickle card.

Evan draws a card. Now he has a burger, bacon, and mustard. Tanner has a bun and cheese, and he draws a burger card.

It's Cole's turn again. He draws a burger. He has a complete hamburger with two other item cards. He lays it all down on the table. He has nine points total. Jordan has five points but he must subtract two points. Evan has negative six points and Tanner has one point.

Each person writes his score on a piece of paper before playing another round.

Make a Hamburger

Quiz

Read the directions to the game. Read the story.

Use the directions and the story to answer the questions.

1. Tanner *shuffled* the cards.
   - Ⓐ He mixed up the cards.
   - Ⓑ He walked slowly to another place with the cards.
   - Ⓒ He moved the cards to the table.
   - Ⓓ He separated the cards into two piles.

2. This story is mainly about
   - Ⓐ a barbecue
   - Ⓑ a hamburger card game
   - Ⓒ a list of food items
   - Ⓓ a group of boys

3. Which of these is an item not usually found on a hamburger?
   - Ⓐ cheese
   - Ⓑ pickle
   - Ⓒ onion
   - Ⓓ ham

4. Think about how the word *cheese* relates to the word *hamburger*. Which words relate in the same way?

   cheese : hamburger

   - Ⓐ card : deck
   - Ⓑ draw : discard
   - Ⓒ points : win
   - Ⓓ lettuce : tomato

5. When someone wins, the other players must
   - Ⓐ eat a hamburger
   - Ⓑ give the winner all the cards
   - Ⓒ subtract points for their items
   - Ⓓ draw more cards

#8864 Informational Reading   ©Teacher Created Resources, Inc.

Guess My Word

New Words

These are new words to practice.
Say each word 10 times.

* guess
* prepare
* alphabet
* hidden

* process
* eliminate
* secret
* none

Choose one new word to write.

Guess My Word

Story

Word Game

Players: two people

Object: to guess your opponent's word

Equipment: lined paper, pencils

Preparation:

Fold your paper in half lengthwise. On each side of the paper at the top draw four horizontal lines. Write each letter of the alphabet down the left side of the paper. Tear a slit along the fold line from the top of the paper about two inches down.

How to play:

Write a four letter word on the lines on one side at the top of the page. Write one letter on each line. Fold that half of the paper down one inch from the top. Fold over again. This will keep your word hidden from the other player.

Players take turns guessing four letter words. One player guesses a word. The other person says how many of the letters in that word are also in her hidden word. Use the alphabet to cross out letters in a process of elimination.

Denise taught her friend Gail how to play a word game. They each got a piece of lined paper and a pencil. They folded their papers, wrote lines across the top, and folded down one side to hide their words. They wrote the letters of the alphabet down the left side of the page. They wrote one letter on each line of the paper.

Denise wrote her secret word. She chose the word "tall." Gail's first guess for Denise was "rock." Denise said zero, to tell Gail her guess has none of the same letters that are in Denise's hidden word. Gail knows she can cross out the letters "r," "o," "c," and "k" on her alphabet list. Those letters are not in Denise's word.

The girls play for a long time. Finally, Denise guesses Gail's word correctly.

Guess My Word

Quiz

**Read the game directions. Read the story.
Use the directions and the story to answer the questions.**

1. How many letters can Denise have in her secret word?
   - (A) five
   - (B) four
   - (C) six
   - (D) seven

2. Denise's *opponent* is the person
   - (A) winning in a contest
   - (B) who disagrees with her
   - (C) playing against her in a game
   - (D) who sits across the room at school

3. This story is mainly about
   - (A) writing letters and words
   - (B) tearing your paper
   - (C) guessing a word
   - (D) being friends

4. Why did Denise fold down half of the paper?
   - (A) to read the back
   - (B) to hide her word
   - (C) to write the alphabet
   - (D) to follow the directions

5. Think about how the word *letter* relates to the word *word*. Which words relate in the same way?

   letter : word

   - (A) word : sentence
   - (B) pencil : paper
   - (C) hide : secret
   - (D) zero : none

Challenge

New Words

These are new words to practice.
Say each word 10 times.

* challenge   * opponent

* normal   * claim

* remove   * continue

* piece   * block

Choose one new word to write.

Challenge

Story

Board Game

Players: two people

Object: Complete the most four piece rows

Equipment:

- game board
- 12 white "normal" playing pieces
- 12 black "normal" playing pieces
- 2 red "removal" pieces
- 2 yellow "removal" pieces
- 2 blue "wild" pieces

How to play:

The game board has 64 squares, set in 8 rows and columns of 8 squares each. One player uses white and red game pieces. The other player uses black and yellow pieces. Each person has one blue "wild" piece.

Players take turns placing on piece at a time on the game board. The object is to place four pieces in a row. A player may play a normal playing piece, a removal piece, or a wild piece.

A removal piece removes all the pieces within a square around it. It removes your pieces and your opponent's. Once pieces have been removed, those spaces may be filled in again. The removal piece stays there. It is not removed.

A wild piece may be played anywhere. It may be placed over an opponent's piece. The player who plays the wild piece claims that space on the board.

The game continues until both players have played all their normal pieces. The player with the most rows of four pieces wins.

Weston and Amber play a game. They received the game from their grandma. The game has a board and various game pieces. The game does not seem difficult to play.

Weston places one of his black pieces on the board. Amber takes her turn. After a few turns, Amber blocks Weston's row with one of her normal pieces.

Weston plays a removal piece next to Amber's row. Any pieces on a square touching the space with Weston's removal piece must be taken off the board. Amber loses two of her pieces and Weston loses one.

Amber's row is close to Weston's. Soon she can play her wild piece and claim a space as hers. Then she will have one complete row of four pieces.

The game continues until they have both used all their pieces. Amber has one row of four. Weston has two complete rows of four pieces. He wins the game.

Challenge

Quiz

Read the game directions. Read the story.

Use the directions and the story to answer the questions.

1. This game is mainly about
   - Ⓐ placing playing pieces in a row
   - Ⓑ coloring playing pieces
   - Ⓒ throwing away game pieces
   - Ⓓ having a wild party

2. What color are Weston's normal pieces?
   - Ⓐ white
   - Ⓑ red
   - Ⓒ yellow
   - Ⓓ black

3. Think about how the word *yellow* relates to the word *color*. Which words relate in the same way?

   | yellow : color |

   - Ⓐ black : white
   - Ⓑ square : shape
   - Ⓒ person : player
   - Ⓓ normal : wild

4. When Amber claims a square,
   - Ⓐ she can put one of her pieces in that space
   - Ⓑ she tells the truth
   - Ⓒ she builds a house on the square
   - Ⓓ she wins the game

5. When Weston plays a wild piece
   - Ⓐ he wins the game
   - Ⓑ he jumps up and down
   - Ⓒ he claims that space as his
   - Ⓓ he takes all his opponent's pieces

Settling the West

New Words

These are new words to practice.
Say each word 10 times.

* cursor   * settler

* click   * oxen

* reach   * difficult

* obstacle   * position

Choose one new word to write.

_____

- - - - - - - - - - - - - - - - - -

_____

Settling the West

Story

Computer Game

Players: one or two players

Object: To reach the Missouri River with the most points.

Set up:
1. put disk in computer
2. select one or two person game
3. move cursor to the correct circle
4. click the mouse button

How to play:

The first player has the character of Johnny Appleseed. He wants to plant apple trees across the west. The other character is Sunbonnet Sue. She wants to plant wheat fields.

Both characters face obstacles. Other settlers want to cut down Johnny's trees to build log cabins. They want to feed their horses grass. Their oxen and wagons create deep ruts in the land. This makes it difficult to plant trees and wheat.

Use the cursor movement keys (arrows) to move your character through each screen. Press the # (pound) key to plant a tree or a field of wheat. To run away from oxen, hold down the arrow key in the direction you wish to run. If someone tries to take a tree to build a house, position the cursor directly on the tree. Click on it *before* they start to chop the tree. If a horse eats grass, click on the grass in the horse's mouth. You will be able to plant wheat. A player gets five points for each tree or wheat field planted.

The game continues until a player reaches the Missouri River. The person with the most points wins. For a one person game, check your point total against any previous scores earned.

Kari finished her work at school and is allowed to play a computer game. The class has been reading about early settlers in the west. Kari chooses to play the Johnny Appleseed game.

She turns on the computer and inserts the disk. Kari chooses the one player game. Her character is Johnny Appleseed. Kari quickly presses the pound key to plant a tree. She keeps playing. She overcomes most of the obstacles in her path.

Kari reaches the river with 20 points. The last time she played she got 10 points. Kari did much better this time.

Settling the West

Quiz

Read the game directions. Read the story.

Use the directions and the story to answer the questions.

1. Both characters face *obstacles*. These things
   - (A) keep them from moving
   - (B) prevent them from planting trees or wheat
   - (C) stop the game
   - (D) are items that they have to jump over

2. This story is mainly about
   - (A) wagons and oxen
   - (B) early settlers in the west
   - (C) apple trees
   - (D) log cabins

3. How far will the settlers travel?
   - (A) until they get away from the oxen
   - (B) until they see grass
   - (C) until they get to the mountains
   - (D) until they get to the Missouri River

4. Think about how the word *apple* relates to the word *tree*. Which words relate in the same way?

   apple : tree

   - (A) build : cabin
   - (B) east : west
   - (C) wheat : field
   - (D) horses : oxen

5. How can Kari get away from the oxen?
   - (A) run away using the arrow key
   - (B) turn off the game
   - (C) get another player to help
   - (D) click the cursor on the oxen

©Teacher Created Resources, Inc.   137   #8864 Informational Reading

Young Rabbit's Journey

New Words

These are new words to practice.
Say each word 10 times.

* marker
* constructed
* burrow
* divide

* equal
* freeze
* zigzag
* evade

Choose one new word to write.

Young Rabbit's Journey

Story

Outdoor Game

Players: a group of people may play

Object: to get from the burrow to Uncle's house

Equipment:

field

markers (cones, string, blocks of wood, etc.)

letter or baton

flags (may be constructed of sticks and fabric scraps)

How to play:

Divide players equally into two teams. Each person may take a name as a dog or a rabbit. There will be at least three rabbits: Father Rabbit, Young Rabbit, and Uncle. Place markers to show places.

rabbit burrow	blackberry bushes

bridge	river

Uncle's house

Place flags to identify dogs' houses.

Father Rabbit gives Young Rabbit the letter for Uncle. Young Rabbit must safely carry the letter to Uncle's burrow.

The other rabbits give Young Rabbit lessons. They tell him how to freeze and zigzag. They teach him to splash through the river and hide in blackberries.

Young Rabbit crosses the field. He goes through town. Dogs will try to catch Young Rabbit. He will try to evade Dogs.

Samuel and his friends enjoy reading books. They like to act out the stories at recess. They make each story into a game.

This week Samuel's class read *Rabbit Hill* by Ben Lawson. This story sounds like a great game to play outside! Samuel and Toby write down ideas for how to play the game.

They can have two teams, dogs and rabbits. They will use flags to mark the dogs' houses. All the players on the rabbit team can help teach Young Rabbit tricks. All the rabbits will be able to zigzag, run into blackberry bushes, freeze, or splash in the river.

The dogs will all try to get the rabbits. If a dog tags a rabbit that person will have to go back to the burrow. Players can take turns being Young Rabbit.

Samuel and Toby show the game ideas to their friends. Everyone is excited to play the game at recess.

Young Rabbit's Journey

Quiz

**Read the game directions. Read the story.
Use the directions and the story to answer the questions.**

1. Where is Young Rabbit going on his journey?

   Ⓐ to the river
   Ⓑ a dog's house
   Ⓒ over the bridge
   Ⓓ to Uncle's burrow

2. Young Rabbit lives in a *burrow*. He lives

   Ⓐ by the river bank
   Ⓑ in a borrowed house
   Ⓒ in a hole in the ground
   Ⓓ in the blackberry bushes

3. This story is mainly about

   Ⓐ playing games outside
   Ⓑ chasing rabbits
   Ⓒ delivering a letter
   Ⓓ writing rules

4. Why did Young Rabbit go to Uncle's?

   Ⓐ to have lunch
   Ⓑ to take a letter
   Ⓒ to play at recess
   Ⓓ to splash in the river

5. Think about how the word *rabbit* relates to the word *burrow*. Which words relate in the same way?

   | rabbit : burrow |

   Ⓐ splash : river
   Ⓑ bird : fly
   Ⓒ stories : books
   Ⓓ fox : den

#8864 Informational Reading   140   ©Teacher Created Resources, Inc.

Answer Sheets

Student Name

Title of Reading Passage

1. (a) (b) (c) (d)
2. (a) (b) (c) (d)
3. (a) (b) (c) (d)
4. (a) (b) (c) (d)
5. (a) (b) (c) (d)

Student Name

Title of Reading Passage

1. (a) (b) (c) (d)
2. (a) (b) (c) (d)
3. (a) (b) (c) (d)
4. (a) (b) (c) (d)
5. (a) (b) (c) (d)

Student Name

Title of Reading Passage

1. (a) (b) (c) (d)
2. (a) (b) (c) (d)
3. (a) (b) (c) (d)
4. (a) (b) (c) (d)
5. (a) (b) (c) (d)

Student Name

Title of Reading Passage

1. (a) (b) (c) (d)
2. (a) (b) (c) (d)
3. (a) (b) (c) (d)
4. (a) (b) (c) (d)
5. (a) (b) (c) (d)

Answer Key

Page 11 – Rafael Needs Shoes
1. B
2. D
3. C
4. A
5. B

Page 14 – Money in the Bank
1. C
2. A
3. B
4. C
5. D

Page 17 – Grocery Shopping
1. D
2. B
3. A
4. B
5. B

Page 20 – Going to the Airport
1. C
2. A
3. B
4. D
5. C

Page 23 – A New Skateboard
1. B
2. C
3. D
4. A
5. B

Page 26 – A Night at the Theater
1. A
2. B
3. A
4. C
5. C

Page 29 – A Favorite Place
1. C
2. C
3. A
4. B
5. D

Page 32 – Teamwork
1. C
2. B
3. B
4. D
5. A

Page 35 – Reminder from Mom
1. B
2. A
3. C
4. A
5. D

Page 38 – Scout Camp
1. C
2. D
3. B
4. B
5. D

Page 41 – Party Time
1. B
2. C
3. A
4. D
5. C

Page 44 – State Report
1. C
2. B
3. D
4. A
5. D

Page 47 – First Day
1. B
2. B
3. C
4. B
5. A

Page 50 – Build a Kite
1. C
2. B
3. A
4. D
5. D

Page 53 – Pancake Breakfast
1. B
2. C
3. B
4. C
5. A

Page 56 – Crazy Hair
1. D
2. B
3. C
4. A
5. C

Page 59 – Adopt a Pet
1. B
2. C
3. A
4. C
5. D

Page 62 – Stay Healthy
1. D
2. B
3. C
4. B
5. A

Answer Key (cont.)

Page 65 – Getting Ready for Fall
1. C
2. D
3. A
4. C
5. B

Page 68 – Movie Time
1. A
2. B
3. B
4. A
5. D

Page 71 – Summer Plans
1. B
2. C
3. D
4. C
5. A

Page 74 – Winter Holiday Concert
1. C
2. A
3. B
4. A
5. D

Page 77 – Gymnastics Class
1. A
2. B
3. C
4. D
5. B

Page 80 – Visit a Volcano
1. B
2. D
3. A
4. B
5. C

Page 83 – Fair Days
1. C
2. B
3. C
4. A
5. D

Page 86 – Friday Night at the Movies
1. A
2. C
3. D
4. C
5. B

Page 89 – Computer Fun
1. B
2. D
3. B
4. A
5. D

Page 92 – Four Wheeling
1. C
2. B
3. C
4. D
5. A

Page 95 – A Modern Artist
1. D
2. A
3. B
4. C
5. B

Page 98 – Technology in the News
1. B
2. C
3. D
4. A
5. A

Page 101 – Anthology of Folk Tales
1. C
2. A
3. B
4. D
5. C

Page 104 – Learning New Science Words
1. B
2. C
3. A
4. B
5. D

Page 107 – At the Lake
1. B
2. D
3. B
4. A
5. B

Page 110 – Exploring the Library
1. C
2. A
3. D
4. B
5. C

Answer Key (cont.)

Page 113 – Shopping Day
1. D
2. B
3. A
4. C
5. B

Page 116 – The World Around Us
1. D
2. B
3. C
4. B
5. A

Page 119 – Steven's New School
1. D
2. B
3. C
4. C
5. A

Page 122 – Sunday Bike Ride
1. C
2. A
3. D
4. B
5. B

Page 125 – Camp Woodleaf
1. B
2. C
3. A
4. C
5. D

Page 128 – Make a Hamburger
1. A
2. B
3. D
4. A
5. C

Page 131 – Guess My Word
1. B
2. C
3. C
4. B
5. A

Page 134 – Challenge
1. A
2. D
3. B
4. A
5. C

Page 137 – Settling the West
1. B
2. B
3. D
4. C
5. A

Page 140 – Young Rabbit's Journey
1. D
2. C
3. A
4. B
5. D